NO SILLY QUESTIONS

NO
SILLY
QU

**THE DAILY AUS EXPLAINS
HOW THE WORLD WORKS
(AND WHY YOU SHOULD CARE)**

ESTIONS

**ZARA SEIDLER &
SAM KOSLOWSKI**

CONTENTS

INTRODUCTION
The media and The Daily Aus 1

1.

OUR POLITICAL SYSTEM
4

A BIG QUESTION
Should 16- and 17-year-olds be allowed to vote? 38

2.

THE ECONOMY
40

A BIG QUESTION
How does HECS work?   70

3.

OUR CLIMATE
72

A BIG QUESTION
What is corporate greenwashing?   100

4.

SOCIETY AND CULTURE
102

A BIG QUESTION
When will we have
a male contraceptive pill?   140

5.

SCIENCE AND TECHNOLOGY
142

A BIG QUESTION
Are vapes harmful
to your health?   176

6.

THE WORLD AROUND US
178

A BIG QUESTION
Should you be able
to erase all your online
personal data?   **208**

CONCLUSION
How to read the news   **211**

A BIG QUESTION
Do we need better
representation
on our screens?   **220**

A FINAL NOTE   **223**
Notes   **226**
Image credits   **227**
About the authors   **229**
Acknowledgements   **230**

INTRODUCTION:
THE MEDIA AND THE DAILY AUS

> Hi! We're Zara and Sam, co-founders of The Daily Aus.

There are no silly questions.
That's where we want to start this news journey with you. With the very simple fact that any question you have about the news is a good one. A worthy one. And we're going to try *really* hard to answer your questions in this book.

The news shouldn't feel overwhelming – overwhelming either because you're struggling to understand some of the key ideas that lie behind a recent development ('Why would I care about interest rates going up when I don't know why interest rates matter?') or because you're reading so much that it's all getting on top of you.

The news can, in fact, feel like a space you're meant to be in – a space where it's okay for ideas to develop, to be challenged, and where no question is a silly one.

'Why are two twenty-somethings telling me how to feel about the news?' we hear you mutter from the other side of this book. A very good question, dear reader.

Well, the answer is that we have been trying, for the past few years, to build a media company that makes *everyone* feel like news is for them. Even if they're not 'news people'.

Building The Daily Aus

In 2017, we started The Daily Aus. The mission back then, and the one that still drives us today, was to create a news service that empowers young people to engage with the world around them. For years, we'd heard things like, 'Young people are lazy' and 'They don't realise how good they've got it.'

Yet, when we were talking to our friends, all in their twenties, the reality was different. Many felt like there was nowhere for them to get information that was clear, concise and in their language. Importantly, they weren't out buying papers or surfing the web, and there were no news outlets catering to a social-first generation.

And so, The Daily Aus was born. The antidote to the opinion-first, noisy news cycle. A digestible and bite-sized way to consume news, which explained the context behind a story, not just the headline of the day. We weren't trying to make people change their daily routines or consumption habits. Instead, we wanted to meet young people where they were, and ensure that accurate and factual news was intercepting people mid-doomscroll.

At the beginning, that looked like uploading five news items to Instagram stories every single day, despite both of us working in other jobs. Crucially, the fifth story of every 'bulletin' would be a good news story, ensuring the reader ended each interaction with 'the news' on a positive note. In those early days, though our audience remained *very* small, they were phenomenally engaged. This was our training ground – where we learnt what young people need from their news, how they best understand complex ideas, what traditional outlets expect them to know, and how an issue moves from being a story for the diehard current-affairs consumer to a part of everyday conversations we want to take part in.

When the COVID-19 pandemic hit, we knew what to do. We knew we had to bring the same level of clarity to pandemic news as we had to other stories, and that we had to make sense of a seemingly incomprehensible news event for our audience. Rightly or wrongly, the pandemic forced everyone – regardless of their age, socio-economic status, race or religion – to pay attention to the news. Suddenly, news outlets had the answers about where you could go, who you could see and what you could do.

The exponential growth of our audience was a huge responsibility that we didn't take lightly. We wanted to get it right for them, keep them informed with the facts, but also identify when something was 'noise' and not 'news'. It was about toeing the line between informing and overwhelming, and it relied on us listening and responding to our audience.

Today, that audience has grown considerably, with The Daily Aus reaching over one million young Australians every month. We have a daily podcast, newsletter, TikTok, video channel, website . . . and now, a book.

Our intention for this book is for it to be the world's best cheat sheet for understanding how the world works. Think of it like a friend in your pocket that you can whip out to explain all the big concepts in life, but in a way that makes sense to *you*.

One challenge with writing the book is the ever-changing nature of news. We know how fast things move – from changes in governments and regimes around the world to understanding pandemics, science and technology. We've tried to include explainers that will stay relevant and to which you can refer when you need to brush up on a topic.

Part of the problem – and therefore part of the reason we wanted to write this book – is that most of us weren't really taught a lot of this stuff growing up. Unless you took an economics subject at high school or university, it's not easy to understand superannuation, tax, GST, inflation, GDP, interest rates, tariffs or currencies. That's not your fault. But it's a problem that can be fixed by taking time to read explainers on the big questions you might feel silly asking (or don't even know how to go about asking).

So, we hope you can use this book when you're reading a news story about climate change, politics, technology, war or money. Keep it handy and come back to a specific chapter when you need to.

For now, make yourself a cup of tea, find yourself a sunny spot, and let's get to all your questions – even the ones you might think are silly.

OUR
POLI[T]
SYST[E]

1.

**ICAL
EM**

WHY SHOULD I CARE ABOUT OUR POLITICAL SYSTEM?

We're kicking off with politics. There are *lots* of good reasons to care about politics. The decisions made by politicians have enormous implications for our quality of life today. They also shape the world of tomorrow.

And just as it's your quality of life on the line, it's also your money. If you earn money in Australia and therefore pay tax, your tax dollars pay for the policies announced in Canberra – not to mention the salary of the politicians announcing them.

But, for us, the biggest reason you should care about politics can be summed up in one word: *privilege*.

It is a privilege to live in a country that has free, democratic elections. It is a privilege to feel safe when voting. It is a privilege to have access to independent media reporting on politics. There are millions of people around the world who don't have these privileges, and they shouldn't be taken for granted.

Politics can be tricky to follow. It's fast-paced, and political reporting often relies on the consumer having a lot of assumed knowledge. That is exactly what we want to avoid. We're here to demystify politics for you, so that next time you're reading news about a leadership spill, a ministerial appointment or a new policy, you'll understand the full picture.

That's vital when you think about who our politicians and political processes are created to serve: you. Politicians are elected to represent the interests of all Australians, every single day. Following politics is how you can try to ensure they do that job well.

Our hope with this chapter is that if you've said things in the past like 'Politics doesn't matter to me' or 'It makes no difference to my life what politicians do,' you'll realise the opposite is in fact true. Politics touches all of us, and the more you know, the more power you have.

Before we jump into it, a quick note. There are three levels of government in Australia: local, state and federal. In this chapter, we're focusing on making sense of the federal political system. That's because it is nationally consistent, meaning whether you're reading this in Western Australia or New South Wales, Queensland or the Northern Territory, the facts will remain the same for you.

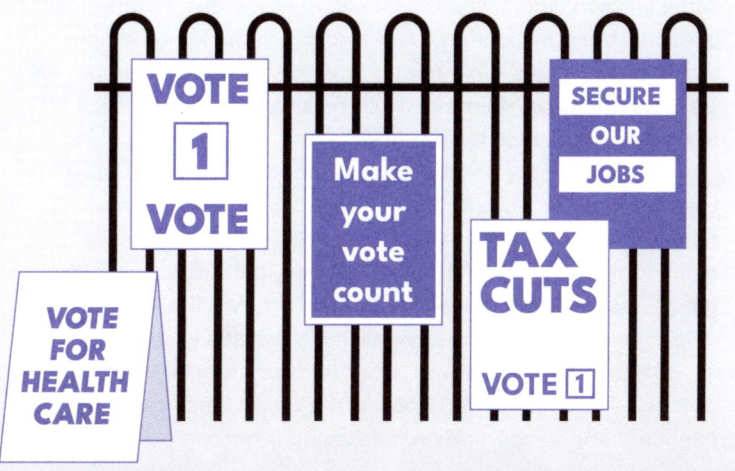

HAVE YOUR SAY: HOW WE PARTICIPATE IN POLITICS

Smell that? That, friends, is the scent of participating in democracy (mixed with that iconic Australian democracy sausage sizzling outside the polling place). Even if you pay very little attention to politics in your day-to-day life, if you are eighteen or older and live in Australia, there's a high chance you have voted in an election. Voting is the most obvious entry point to participating in our political system – and, in Australia, it's compulsory. So it's the most obvious place to start our chapter.

Why is voting compulsory?

Compulsory voting was introduced in Australia in 1924, after there had been a decline in voter turnout following World War I.

As a method of ensuring more people voted, it worked. In 1922, less than 60 per cent of Australians voted. In 1925, after compulsory voting became law, more than 90 per cent of Australians voted.

It's interesting to note that, by international standards, compulsory voting is extremely rare – there are fewer than twenty-five countries in the world where voting is compulsory. So, is it a good thing or a bad thing?

It depends on who you ask. Some people argue that compulsory voting produces a 'better indication of the opinion of the people than voluntary voting', while others argue that with compulsory voting, 'we do not know how many people give consideration to their votes'.[1]

There are a couple of things we think are interesting about compulsory voting. First, it changes the national conversation come election time. In the US, for example, millions, if not billions, of dollars are spent during every election campaign on simply trying to convince eligible people to vote. In the 2020 presidential election, about two-thirds of US citizens voted, which was the highest turnout of the twenty-first century.

By comparison, in the last Australian federal election, in 2022, voter turnout was close to 90 per cent. In Australia, our focus isn't on ensuring people do vote, it's about ensuring people have an informed vote. That's still a hell of a task, but it does arguably get us closer to being sure the winning party has the support of the greatest share of the people it is supposed to represent.

Second, having a compulsory voting system means successful parties need to appeal to a broad cross-section of Australians. In countries where voting is not compulsory, this isn't always the case. When Donald Trump was elected US president in 2016, he won about 46 per cent of the votes of those who cast a ballot, but only 27 per cent of those who were eligible to vote (i.e. including those who stayed home).

Why does this need for broad appeal matter? Well, it means the major parties in Australia must have policies that are closer to the centre of public opinion, whereas parties in the US and other places where voting is not compulsory have space for their policies to be more extreme.

Whether you consider these consequences to be good or bad is entirely up to you! But let's get down to business. You have to vote, so how does it work?

Preferential voting

It's election day. You've visited the cake stall or sausage sizzle and it's time to vote.

In fact, it's time to vote twice. We have two jobs on election day. First, to elect a representative for our local area (or electorate), who will sit in the House of Representatives (called a Member of Parliament or MP). Second, we elect several representatives for our state or territory to sit in the Senate. We'll come back to what those two bodies do later on. First, the logistics.

For the House of Representatives, you'll be given a green ballot listing every candidate running in your electorate. One of those candidates will be elected using the preferential voting system.

It's pretty common to hear people talk about who they vote for. But what's sometimes forgotten is that you have to vote for everyone. *Sort of.*

When you vote for the House of Representatives, you need to rank every candidate running in your electorate from first to last.

SCAN ME FOR MORE

It's not just your number one choice that matters, the order matters too. When all the votes get counted, the first step is counting up everyone's #1 vote, or their first 'preference'. Whichever candidate receives the fewest first-preference votes is eliminated. Anybody who voted #1 for that candidate has their vote transferred to the person they put in the #2 spot, or their second preference. Have a look at this video for a TDA breakdown of how votes are counted – using lollies, of course.

PREFERENCE DEALS

Ever heard parties talk about who they're 'preferencing'? This refers to the order they put the parties on their how-to-vote cards.

What's a how-to-vote card?

It's the party-branded sheet of paper volunteers offer you at the voting booth. It will have a suggested order for you to fill out the preferences on your ballot. But that's all it is: a suggestion.

The way you order the candidates on the ballot is your decision. You can't 'accidentally' end up voting for a party or a candidate you don't support because of a preference 'deal' made by a political party or anyone other than you.

2
7
3
→ 1
6
4
5

Proportional representation

Your second job on election day is to vote for senators to represent your state or territory. If you live in a state, you'll have six senators to elect, and if you live in the ACT or the NT, you'll have two.

Whereas MPs must be re-elected at every election (roughly every three years), senators are elected for six-year terms, alternating so that half the seats are up for grabs at each election. Senators for the two territories, the ACT and NT, are the exception – they are re-elected at every election.

There are usually a lot of candidates in the Senate – sometimes more than a hundred in a single state. This means the white Senate ballot paper you get on election day is often extremely long and daunting.

You have two options – voting 'above the line' or voting 'below the line'. Above the line, you'll see a list of all the parties running candidates for the Senate. Below the line, you'll see the names of all the candidates who are running, sorted by their party groups, as well as any candidates not affiliated with a party.

If you choose to vote above the line, you vote for parties. You have to number at least six boxes, but you don't have to number them all. Your preferences will flow first through all the candidates in your first-choice party, then the candidates in your second-choice party and so on.

If you choose to vote below the line, you have to number at least twelve boxes (again, you don't have to do them all). Your preferences will go to individual candidates in the order you have chosen.

Votes for the Senate are counted using a different system to the House of Representatives, called proportional representation. It's notoriously complicated, so buckle up.

One reason it's complicated is because there are multiple 'winners' for each state or territory, not just one like in the House of Representatives. These senators are chosen using a system of quotas – one quota for each position. For a state's six senators, the quota is 14.3 per cent (based on a fancy formula).

Any candidate who gets 14.3 per cent of first-preference votes is automatically elected. Any votes above 14.3 per cent get redistributed among the remaining candidates, and the candidates with the smallest vote shares are gradually eliminated until six senators reach the 14.3 per cent finish line.

This system allows some parties to get multiple senators. If 43 per cent of people in a state vote for Party One above the line, that's enough for three full quotas and Party One's top three candidates will be elected as senators.

But it also means candidates from minor parties can get elected even if they start with only a small number of first-preference votes, because the preferences keep flowing around until six candidates end up with 14.3 per cent, even if some of those candidates had nowhere near that much support to begin with.

Senate ballot paper

You may vote in one of two ways

Either

Above the line
By numbering at least 6 of these boxes in the order of your choice (with number 1 as your first choice)

Or

Below the line
By numbering at least 12 of these boxes in the order of your choice (with number 1 as your first choice)

For example, at the 2022 election, the United Australia Party's Ralph Babet was elected to the Senate despite getting only 4 per cent of first-preference votes. How? The two major parties each received slightly more than 30 per cent, enough to get two senators elected but not enough to get close to a third. The Greens had 13.85 per cent, not quite enough for a full quota on their own but enough to make up the distance quickly with preferences. The rest of the vote was split among a variety of minor parties, leading to a complex preference process which eventually saw Babet succeed.

How does a prime minister get elected?

If you've voted in a federal election, you probably noticed that the two leaders in contention for the prime ministership weren't on your ballot papers (unless you happen to live in their electorate).

That's because, in Australia, we don't directly elect the prime minister. Government is formed by whichever party wins a majority of the 151 seats in the House of Representatives, and that party's leader becomes the prime minister.

A party's leader is typically chosen by their party, not by voters. Some parties allow their MPs and senators to choose a leader, while others also allow members of the public to have a say if they pay a fee to become party members.

But when it comes to election time, the party leaders are campaigning to be local representatives just like any other MP – they don't 'run for PM' in the same way politicians 'run for president' in the US.

Party leaders are still important figures in election campaigns – voting for a local candidate from the leader's party will help that party to win a majority and form government. So it makes sense to consider your opinion of the person who would lead that government when you vote for a local member.

WHAT ABOUT WHEN WE DON'T ELECT THE PRIME MINISTER?

The lowdown on leadership spills

Remember that time between 2010 and 2018 when we had more prime ministers than there were reality TV dating shows? We had Kevin Rudd, Julia Gillard, Kevin Rudd (again), Tony Abbott, Malcolm Turnbull and Scott Morrison all within a matter of years.

A few of these changes were because of something called a leadership spill. The most recent one was in 2018, when Scott Morrison replaced Malcolm Turnbull.

As we've just seen, the prime minister is the leader of whichever party wins the most seats in the House of Representatives. So, if a party decides that it no longer has confidence in its leader, its elected MPs and senators can call for a leadership spill. This is when a party declares that the position of the leader is vacant and open for re-election.

There are different rules for different parties. For example, after Morrison ousted Turnbull, he changed the rules so that an elected Liberal Party leader who is prime minister cannot be removed from office unless at least two-thirds of the party room (which includes all the party's MPs and senators) votes in favour of having a leadership spill.

In the Labor Party, a prime minister cannot be removed unless three-quarters of Labor's caucus agrees to force a ballot. These thresholds for electing a new leader are lower if the party is in opposition.

The constitution and referendums

So, you've navigated our main task as a citizen, voting on election day. Time to put your feet up until the next election, right? Not quite. There's plenty more to do to hold our elected representatives to account for what they do between elections.

First, though, there's one more formal task voters have to do very occasionally: vote on changes to the constitution.

What is a constitution? Basically, it's the highest law of the land. It sets out the roles and limitations of our government and imposes guidelines on the kinds of laws our parliament can pass.

The Constitution of Australia was drafted in the late 1800s and came into effect in 1901. It is the founding document that established Australia as a federation – a mutual agreement of the six pre-existing colonies (Australia's six states) to set up a central government with certain powers.

Because of its foundational nature, the constitution is really, really hard to change. But as you can imagine, there are some parts of this document that was composed more than one hundred years ago that people believe should change to suit modern Australia.

So how do changes happen? The government must hold a referendum, which is a 'yes' or 'no' question put to the Australian people about a proposed change. Unlike an ordinary law, which your parliamentary representatives vote on for you, when it comes to changing the highest law in the land, *you* are the lawmaker.

THE STAT

90.77%

The percentage of people who voted in favour of amending the constitution to include First Nations Peoples in the Census and allow the Commonwealth to make laws for them in the 1967 referendum.

To succeed, a referendum must be approved by a majority of voters across Australia and also a majority of voters in a majority of states. Since Federation in 1901, Australia has had forty-four referendums, with just eight being 'carried' (succeeding) at the time of writing. The referendum with the greatest 'yes' vote was in 1967, when Australians voted yes to First Nations Peoples being counted as part of the population and to giving the federal government power to make laws for First Nations Peoples (rather than only the states).

The last referendum was held in 1999, and asked voters whether to establish Australia as a republic and replace the Queen as our head of state. (More on that below.) It did not succeed.

When the Albanese government won the 2022 election, it committed to holding referendums on two issues – the question of establishing a Voice to Parliament for First Nations Peoples, and the question of whether Australia should become a republic.

ULURU STATEMENT FROM THE HEART

On 26 May 2017, 250 First Nations leaders from across the country gathered to deliver and endorse the Uluru Statement from the Heart. It outlined the path forward for recognising First Nations Peoples in the nation's constitution.

After the First Nations leaders delivered the statement, it was rejected by then-prime minister Malcolm Turnbull. Five years later, its three key elements had still not been implemented.

The first element (the elements are designed to be sequential) is implementing a First Nations Voice to Parliament – an official representative body that would give First Nations Peoples a say in laws and policies that affect them. The Uluru Statement specifically asks for the Voice to Parliament to be enshrined in the Australian constitution, which does not currently recognise First Nations Peoples. This would require a referendum vote.

Once a Voice to Parliament is enshrined in the constitution, the second element in the Uluru Statement asks for a Makarrata Commission to be established. Makarrata is a word in the Yolngu language that means coming together after a struggle; the Makarrata Commission would lead the drafting and signing of a treaty. Australia is the only Commonwealth country that has not signed a treaty with its First Nations Peoples. A treaty is a way of reaching a settlement between First Nations Peoples and those who have colonised their lands.

The last element of the Uluru Statement is truth-telling, which would also be supervised under the Makarrata Commission. Truth-telling would involve the opportunity for First Nations Peoples to share their culture, heritage and history with the broader community. It could involve many aspects, such as altering the curriculum in education settings to provide more accurate learnings about Australia's past.

The head of state

Most governments have three branches – a legislature to make laws, an executive to enact them and a judiciary to interpret them.

Australia's constitution sets out all three of these. Parliament is our law-making body, and the High Court is the top legal authority for interpreting those laws.

What about our executive? You might think the power to enact laws sits under the prime minister. That may be true in practice, but our constitution actually establishes someone else as the head of our executive government, or head of state. That person is the British monarch.

This makes our system of government a constitutional monarchy. Executive power in our system ultimately rests with the British royal family, currently King Charles III. But the king – as you may have noticed – doesn't have any role in the day-to-day running of government. His executive power is carried out by the governor-general, the Crown's representative in Australia.

In turn, the governor-general typically delegates most powers to the elected government of the day and to the parliament. The governor-general formally gives royal assent (approval) to laws that have passed by parliament. A bill does not become law in Australia until this assent is given, and the governor-general can technically approve or reject any law on behalf of the king. However, this does not happen in practice.

There has been one notable exception to this. In 1975, then-governor-general John Kerr intervened in a parliamentary dispute to dismiss an elected government, the Whitlam Labor government.

The republic movement

Whitlam's dismissal was a highly controversial moment in Australian history and gave impetus to the movement in Australia to remove the British monarch as Australia's head of state. This movement is called the republic movement because it seeks to make Australia an independent republic instead of a constitutional monarchy.

Doing this would again require a change to the constitution. Australia had a referendum on this question in 1999, but the majority of Australians voted to keep then-monarch Queen Elizabeth II as Australia's head of state. At the time, around 45 per cent of people voted yes and 55 per cent voted no.

In recent times there has been a renewed push for an Australian republic, especially following the death of Queen Elizabeth II.

Prime Minister Anthony Albanese supports a republic and in 2022 appointed the country's first ever assistant minister for the republic to oversee the issue. That minister was sworn in by the governor-general. (Yes, the governor-general swore in the man who is trying to make his role redundant. Awkward? Never!)

In 2022, the Albanese government said it would consider a second referendum on the question of becoming a republic if it won a second term of government at the 2025 election. The governor-general's role is safe... for now.

Native title

All this talk about British monarchs is an inescapable reminder of Australia's colonial history. We will discuss the legacy of the British invasion of Australia at length in 'Society and Culture'. For now, though, while we're dealing with foundational questions, it's important to cover a vital law introduced by Australia more than thirty years ago which seeks to grapple with that legacy: the *Native Title Act*.

Native title is a legal recognition that First Nations Peoples have continuous and pre-existing rights over their land and waters. It acknowledges that First Nations Peoples lived in Australia for tens of thousands of years prior to British arrival. Native title overturned a colonial notion of terra nullius – the legal concept that deemed Australian land unoccupied or uninhabited.

Native title became law following a 1992 High Court decision in a case brought by Meriam activist Eddie Mabo. After learning that the Mer island in the Torres Strait was owned by the Australian government and not by the Meriam people, he and four other Meriam people launched a legal claim for ownership.

In 1993, the Australian Senate passed the *Native Title Act* following 51 hours and 49 minutes of debate. It gave effect to this High Court decision by setting out a legal framework for First Nations Peoples to claim native title.

Since then, native title has been recognised over more than 32 per cent of Australian land. However, the Australian Institute for Aboriginal and Torres Strait Islander Studies (AIATSIS), a First Nations–led government organisation, has described the system as imperfect. AIATSIS notes the requirements for proving native title are 'significant and burdensome', requiring those who claim native title to provide evidence 'of a continuous system of law and custom that gives rights to the land, and that this has been handed down from generation to generation since before colonisation'.

Native title holders are entitled to compensation for 'activities which diminish or damage their native title rights and interests', but AIATSIS says this area of native title law will likely need to 'develop further' in the years to come, especially when it comes to guidance for compensation claims.[2]

HOW IT ALL GOES DOWN: HOW OUR POLITICAL SYSTEM WORKS

If the big question we're trying to answer in this chapter is how Australia's political system works, then the next place to visit is the one most of us associate with politics: Parliament House. It's the place where we, the people, are represented, and laws are debated and passed.

The physical parliament stands in Canberra, the country's capital city. As we touched on earlier, it has two chambers, the House of Representatives and the Senate. These two houses form the legislature, voting to pass laws. They are also where executive power is wielded by the prime minister and Cabinet ministers, and where the rest of parliament holds these executive leaders accountable.

This system is sometimes dubbed the 'Washminster' system because it combines elements of the US system ('Washington', which has two houses with the same names and similar roles) and the UK system ('Westminster', which has ministers held accountable by parliament). How does it work?

What is the purpose of the House of Reps and the Senate?

HOUSE OF REPRESENTATIVES

Let's start with the House of Representatives, which is also called the 'lower house'. You might recognise this as the green room in parliament where MPs shout at each other during Question Time (apparently they don't teach manners in parliament, Mr Speaker).

The House of Representatives gets its name because every member represents a local community somewhere in the country. Those local communities are grouped into electorates, which vary in size but have roughly similar populations. There are 151 electorates, each with one representative (or one 'seat') in the lower house.

Whoever has a majority of the 151 seats (quick maths, anyone? 76 seats!) is able to form government. The leader of the majority party becomes the prime minister, and other elected representatives from the party are selected by the PM to become ministers in the Cabinet.

But, for now, just remember that the lower house is the house of government: whichever party has the most MPs out of the 151 seats will be the party that runs the country.

SENATE

The Senate is also called the 'upper house'. This is the red room in parliament. There are 76 senators – twelve for each state and two for each of the territories. Every member of the Senate represents their state and territory instead of a specific local community.

If the lower house is the house of government, the upper house is the house that reviews the government. The nature of the Senate voting system means the party with a majority to form government in the House of Reps often does not control a majority in the Senate. This can make the Senate a thorn in a government's side and require it to negotiate with senators from other political parties or from no political party.

WAIT . . . HOW DO YOU PASS LAWS AGAIN?

The lawmaking process begins with a 'bill' – a proposal to create a new law or amend an existing one. Bills are usually introduced in the House of Representatives and then sent to the Senate, but they can also be introduced in the Senate in some cases.

For a bill to become law, both houses must 'pass' it – meaning it must be voted for by the majority of MPs in the lower house and senators in the upper house – in identical form. It's as easy as that! (*Narrator: It is not easy.*)

OUR POLITICAL SYSTEM

WHO ARE THE MAJOR POLITICAL PARTIES IN AUSTRALIA?

The three most prominent parties in Australia are the Labor Party, the Liberal Party and the National Party. At the federal level, the Liberal Party and the National party form what is known as the Coalition.

When the Coalition is in power, the leader of the Liberal Party takes the role of prime minister and the leader of the National Party becomes deputy prime minister. The Liberals (usually the larger of the parties) have never formed government without the National Party's support, so Australia's system can basically be treated as a 'two-party system': for several decades, either Labor or the Coalition has been in government and the other in opposition.

While no political parties are uniform blocs, for the purposes of giving you a broad understanding of the political landscape, here's a general summary of what the parties stand for.

LABOR PARTY

The Labor Party is traditionally the party of working people. It has its roots in the union movement and exists to push for economic changes that benefit workers, such as increasing the minimum wage.

Labor is considered the more socially progressive of the two major parties. A recent example of this is Labor's support for implementing the Uluru Statement from the Heart, which some conservatives do not support.

A common way to define political parties is on a 'spectrum' between left and right, where the left is more socially progressive and favours the government playing a more active role in our lives, and the right is the opposite. On this spectrum, the Labor Party is considered centre left.

Some recent prime ministers from the Labor Party include Kevin Rudd, Julia Gillard, Kevin Rudd (again...) and Anthony Albanese.

LIBERAL PARTY

The Liberal Party is traditionally the party of business. It tends to push for economic changes that benefit businesses and their owners. It believes the government should have minimal interference in our daily lives, prioritising individual freedom and responsibility. It also tends to be more socially conservative than Labor.

On the political spectrum, the Liberal Party is considered centre right. Recent prime ministers from the Liberal Party include Tony Abbott, Malcolm Turnbull and Scott Morrison.

THE NATIONALS

WHAT ABOUT THE NATIONALS?

The National Party is technically a minor party, but gets to participate in governments because of its alliance with the Liberal Party.

The National Party is traditionally the party for regional Australia. The Nationals are typically considered further to the right than the Liberal party, especially on social issues. Some prominent recent leaders of the National Party include Barnaby Joyce, Michael McCormack, Barnaby Joyce (yes, again...) and David Littleproud.

WHO ARE THE MINOR POLITICAL PARTIES IN AUSTRALIA?

We've outlined who the major parties are, but as we noted earlier, your vote isn't limited to these options.

In fact, historical trends show that voters are becoming less and less likely to give their first preference to the major parties. In 1949, the Labor, Liberal and National parties secured about 96 per cent of the House of Representatives first-preference vote. In the 2022 election, just 68 per cent of Australians voted for one of those three parties as their first preference.

So, who are the minor parties capturing voters' attention?

THE GREENS

The minor party with the largest representation in Australian politics is the Greens. In fact, in recent elections, the Greens have attracted significantly more votes than the National Party.

The Greens are on the left of the political spectrum and are known for their socially progressive policies. These include more ambitious emissions reduction targets to combat climate change, building more social housing, including dental treatment under Medicare, free early-childhood care, fee-free TAFE and university education, and a treaty with First Nations Peoples.

The Greens often say their aim is to win the balance of power in both houses – that is, to win enough seats that a government (most likely Labor) would need their support to pass any law opposed by the opposition.

THE UNITED AUSTRALIA PARTY

The United Australia Party (UAP) was founded by mining and real estate billionaire Clive Palmer and is on the far right of the political spectrum. UAP's policies have changed over time, but in the most recent election the party was mainly focused on opposing COVID vaccine mandates and other pandemic measures.

You might have heard of the UAP if you received an unsolicited text message from them during the 2022 election campaign. That's what the party is most known for: spending tens of millions of dollars on advertising and marketing. But money can't buy everything. In the 2019 election, the UAP did not secure a single seat in the House of Reps or the Senate, while in 2022 it won a single Senate seat – an expensive endeavour.

ONE NATION

One Nation, also known as Pauline Hanson's One Nation (PHON), is another minor party you might hear a lot about, not necessarily because of their representation in parliament but because of their high-profile leader (you guessed it: Pauline Hanson).

One Nation holds two seats in the Senate, one of which is held by Hanson herself. It is also a far-right party, best known for its anti-immigration stance. One Nation says it favours 'Australians first and foremost', and believes in reducing Australia's refugee intake.

INDEPENDENTS

Independents are politicians or candidates who are not affiliated with any party. If an independent candidate is successful at winning a seat in the House of Reps or the Senate, they enter parliament and sit on the crossbench (see below) alongside members of minor parties.

In the 2022 election, independents overall proved to be successful, winning ten of the 151 seats in the lower house.

What's the crossbench?

The crossbench refers to any MPs and senators who are not from either of the major parties. The Greens are on the crossbench. So is One Nation, and so are the independents.

- GOVERNMENT
- OPPOSITION
- CROSSBENCH

When a government has a majority of seats in its own right, the votes of crossbenchers are less consequential, because the government doesn't need to win them over in order to pass legislation.

Historically, in Australia, crossbenchers are more powerful in the Senate, where it is less likely for one party to have a clear majority. At the time of writing, there are eighteen senators on the Senate crossbench.

But House of Reps crossbenchers can be crucial too, when neither major party has enough seats to govern in its own right. This situation is called a hung parliament, and whichever party governs in a hung parliament forms a minority government.

How does minority government work? The party that wants to govern needs to secure an agreement from enough crossbenchers to make up the difference to 76 seats (for example, a party with 70 seats would need to secure the support of six crossbenchers).

This support doesn't have to come in the form of a formal coalition – usually, the crossbenchers just need to sign an agreement saying they will support the government on key economic bills that enable the party to spend money and keep the wheels of government turning. This is known as guaranteeing supply. You can think of it as their crossbenchers giving their blessing to one of the major parties to form government, while retaining their right to vote however they like on contentious issues.

In this scenario, crossbenchers don't usually give away their support without strings attached – they can use their position to leverage the government into acting on causes they care about.

An example of this was when Julia Gillard's Labor government needed support from the Greens and other independents to form government and get legislation passed after the 2010 election, which meant the Greens were able to push for strong carbon emissions policies. This resulted in Australia's short-lived *Clean Energy Act* (short-lived because it was repealed a few years later when the Coalition came to power).

Sometimes people say a hung parliament can make it harder to get laws passed, considering the government doesn't have an outright majority in the lower house. However, this isn't always the case. The Gillard minority government had one of the highest rates of passing legislation in Australian history, despite governing in minority with the support of Greens and independents.[3]

What are party factions?

So far, we've focused on how parties (and the occasional independent) deal with one another. But parties themselves are not always uniform. In fact, they can often be split into defined subgroups called 'factions'.

Factions are something real political nerds (*cough* *us* *cough*) care about a lot, but they aren't necessarily something the general public will hear much about, considering that most political parties would like to present as unified a front as possible.

You know how when you go to a party, there are a lot of small groups all having discussions in their separate corners? That's basically what factions are. In politics, they are smaller groups within a party that share closer ties than the group at large. They exist at both the state and federal level, and in both the Liberal and Labor parties.

Factions are typically formed around political interests, although sometimes they are also centred on personalities.

Factions tend to be most important when a party is choosing a new leader. Factions will do deals with each other – one faction might say to another faction, if you let one of us become leader, we'll let one of you be the deputy leader. Factional deals happen in the course of normal parliamentary business too. One faction might offer to compromise on legislation to keep another faction happy if they need something else down the road.

Think about it like this: any large group of people will contain differences of opinion, and factions are just a way to formalise these differences. For example, the two major groupings in the Labor Party are called the 'left' and 'right'. The two major groupings in the Liberal Party are 'moderates' (closer to the political centre) and 'conservatives'. Factions allow these groups to negotiate with one another to find a middle ground – kind of like a parliament within a parliament.

The business of governing: what is a Cabinet?

In Australia's system, the prime minister is appointed by the governor-general to carry out the executive business of government. Prime ministers do this by appointing a Cabinet made up of ministers. Ministers are senior members of the governing party or coalition, typically drawn from both the lower and upper house. Each has a different area of government policy (called a portfolio) to oversee. For example, we have a minister for women, a minister for foreign affairs and a minister for climate change.

Ministers are the government's main decision-makers. They are responsible for proposing new laws in their portfolios and also often have executive powers. For example, the immigration minister has the power to personally cancel a visa and the environment minister has the power to cancel a construction project if it could damage the environment.

During a government's three-year term, it is normal for there to be some reshuffling of portfolios. One question we often get asked is, how does someone go from being minister for education to minister for agriculture? Don't you need to be an expert in the field you are creating laws for?

The simple answer is no. Just as you don't need any formal qualifications to become a politician, there are none required to become a minister. The truth is that ministerial appointments are more often political than they are based on expertise.

However, even if the ministers aren't experts themselves to begin with, they are certainly surrounded by those with expert knowledge to advise them. During the pandemic, then-health minister Greg Hunt didn't have a medical degree – he relied on briefings and advice from then-chief medical officer Professor Brendan Murphy, a former nephrologist (kidney specialist), who was in turn supported by the Department of Health, staffed by thousands of public servants with health system expertise.

One thing to clear up before we move on: the Cabinet is different from the relatively newer body known as the National Cabinet. This is a meeting between the prime minister and state and territory leaders, established in March 2020 to respond to the COVID-19 pandemic. In 2020, then-prime minister Scott Morrison announced National Cabinet would continue beyond the pandemic, replacing a similar forum called the Council of Australian Governments (COAG).

Diversity in gover[nment...]
It allows for a gre[ater...]
perspectives info[rming...]
making. It allows [...]
government touc[hes...]
budgets to domes[tic...]
and from environm[ental...]
to cultural funding[...]
through a multidi[mensional...]

ment matters.
 variety of
ing the decision-
ry topic the
 – from federal
 violence policies,
ntal regulation
 to be viewed
nsional lens.

REPRESENTATION OF WOMEN IN POLITICS

So, there are factions, there is a Cabinet and there's a crossbench. But who are the people occupying those spaces? The long and short of it is they have traditionally been men. But that's changing.

Has anyone else found themselves in an argument about quotas? It's an issue that riles people up in many fields, and politics is no exception.

Quotas are designed to address the unequal participation of women and members of minority groups in areas of society where they are traditionally under-represented, including politics. Broadly, a quota involves setting a certain number or percentage of places that must be occupied by under-represented groups.

According to the International Parliamentary Union, in 2022 Australia ranked 57th in the world for women's representation in parliament.[4] Our position on this ranking system has actually declined over the past twenty years – despite the proportion of women in the lower house (which is what the ranking is based on) increasing, other countries have made significantly more progress than us in the same period of time.

Of course, the under-representation of women in politics is not an issue specific to Australia. A 2018 investigation by the *New York Times* found there were more men named John who were senators in the Republican Party (one of the two major parties in the US) than there were women. This was despite the fact that men named John made up about 3 per cent of the male population in the US, and women made up about 51 per cent of the total US population.[5]

One example of somewhere quotas have worked is the United Arab Emirates, which has legislated a quota for women's political representation. In 1997, its parliament had no women. In 2022, it has 50 per cent female representation.

In Australia, we don't have any mandatory quotas, but parties can choose to set them for themselves. In federal politics, the Labor Party has had quotas for women in some form since 1994. The Coalition does not have any quota systems in place.

In the 47th Parliament, 52 per cent of Labor MPs and senators are women. For the Coalition, this number is 27 per cent. (According to the 2021 Census, 50.7 per cent of the Australian population are women and 49.3 per cent are men, although the Census did not collect data on gender diversity.)

Those who oppose quotas say people should get their jobs purely based on merit and claim gender quotas have the potential to be discriminatory against men. Quotas could mean that some women or members of an under-represented group would be perceived as getting a job only because they fill a quota.

Proponents of quotas say that, as it stands, people aren't getting jobs based on merit anyway. If they were, there would be more women and minority groups in the top jobs. Australia wouldn't have only had one female prime minister in more than 120 years of government.

A 2013 Australian parliamentary review found gender quotas to be 'the most effective mechanism for increasing women's political representation'.[6]

KEY POLITICAL FIGURES WHO MIGHT COME UP IN CONVERSATION

Edmund Barton
PROTECTIONIST PARTY
1st PRIME MINISTER
1901–1903

WHY DO I CARE?
- Australia's first prime minister, and one of the lead campaigners for Australian Federation.
- Resigned from office to become one of the first judges of the High Court, a role he held until his death in 1920.

Ben Chifley
LABOR PARTY
16th PRIME MINISTER
1945–1949

WHY DO I CARE?
- Australia's prime minister after WWII, who served in the John Curtin Labor government during the war and replaced Curtin when he died in office.
- Broadened immigration and expanded the federal government's role in the economy.

Robert Menzies
LIBERAL PARTY
12th PRIME MINISTER
1939–1941
1949–1966

WHY DO I CARE?
- Longest-serving prime minister in Australia's history – his two periods in office totalled 18 years and 5 months.
- Helped to create the modern Liberal Party.

Harold Holt
LIBERAL PARTY
17th PRIME MINISTER
1966–1967

WHY DO I CARE?

- Initiated Australia's involvement in the Vietnam War, introduced decimal currency (dollars and cents replacing pounds and pence) and was PM during the 1967 referendum, which saw a strong 'Yes' vote to change the constitution to count First Nations Peoples in the national Census.

- Holt's name often comes up because of the mysterious circumstances of his death. In 1967 he went for a swim at a rough Victorian surf beach and was never seen again.

WHY DO I CARE?

- Introduced the first iteration of universal health insurance (then called Medibank, today known as Medicare) in Australia.
- Oversaw Australia's withdrawal from the Vietnam War.
- Abolished the White Australia policy.
- The only Australian prime minister to be dismissed from office by the governor-general.

Gough Whitlam
LABOR PARTY
21st PRIME MINISTER
1972–1975

Bob Hawke
LABOR PARTY
23rd PRIME MINISTER
1983–1991

WHY DO I CARE?

- Held the highest popularity rating of any prime minister since the introduction of public opinion polls.
- Brought together unions and employer groups to resolve a major dispute in a process known as 'The Accords'.
- Well known for his ability to scull beers.

WHY DO I CARE?

- Long-serving treasurer under Bob Hawke who replaced him as prime minister.
- Introduced the National Superannuation Scheme, making retirement savings compulsory in Australia.
- Passed Australia's first native title legislation.

1991–1996
24th PRIME MINISTER

Paul Keating
LABOR PARTY

WHY DO I CARE?

- Responsible for the biggest gun reform in Australia's history, which saw the buyback of privately owned guns following the 1996 Port Arthur massacre.
- Committed Australia to wars in Iraq and Afghanistan.
- Second longest-serving prime minister in Australian history.

1996–2007
25th PRIME MINISTER

John Howard
LIBERAL PARTY

WHY DO I CARE?

- First (and, to date, only) female prime minister in Australia's history.
- Delivered the now-famous 'misogyny speech' in parliament, where she told then–opposition leader Tony Abbott she would 'not be lectured about sexism and misogyny by this man'.
- Introduced the National Disability Insurance Scheme (NDIS).

2010–2013
27th PRIME MINISTER

Julia Gillard
LABOR PARTY

'I rise to oppose the motion moved by the Leader of the Opposition, and in so doing I say to the Leader of the Opposition: I will not be lectured about sexism and misogyny by this man. I will not. The government will not be lectured about sexism and misogyny by this man. Not now, not ever.

The Leader of the Opposition says that people who hold sexist views and who are misogynists are not appropriate for high office. Well, I hope the Leader of the Opposition has got a piece of paper and he is writing out his resignation, because if he wants to know what misogyny looks like in modern Australia, he does not need a motion in the House of Representatives; he needs a mirror. That is what he needs.'

An excerpt of Julia Gillard's 'misogyny speech', delivered 9 October 2012

You can't be what you can't see, right? For generations of Australians, diversity in the halls of Parliament House has been a glaring issue. Australia has, for decades, lagged significantly behind the US, the UK, Canada and Aotearoa New Zealand. For example, a 2018 report from the Australian Human Rights Commission found only 4 per cent of federal MPs had non-European ancestry, compared with 19 per cent of the Australian population.

When the 47th Parliament was sworn in after the 2022 election, it finally felt a little different – not just in the ethnic diversity of our government, but in the gender, cultural, socio-economic background and religious diversity of MPs and senators. There's change in the water in Canberra, and Australia's parliament is slowly starting to look like the people it serves to represent. In fact, the 2022 election ushered in the most diverse parliament in history.

Many will remember 2021 and 2022 as years dominated by the stories and voices of women, and that momentum didn't stop at the gates of Parliament House. The 2022 election saw the proportion of women in politics grow dramatically, resulting in 38 per cent of the House of Representatives and 57 per cent of the Senate being women – a record for both chambers.

THE BRIGHT SIDE

That 4 per cent from a non-European background became 6.6 per cent – still a long way behind the Australian population, but a step in the right direction.

There were now eight First Nations senators in the upper house, and three First Nations MPs in the House of Representatives.

That election saw a surge of independents enter the parliament. These independents, most of whom were women, built their campaigns around community movements. In the New South Wales electorate of Fowler, popular local councillor and deputy mayor Dai Le became the first independent to ever win the seat. In her maiden speech, Le, who came to Australia as a refugee from Vietnam, said: 'This migration story belongs to all of us. It's our story, and we can all be proud to share it.'[7]

This cohort of independents – who many commentators predicted would have no success at the election – dramatically changed the face of politics in this country.

Diversity in government matters. It allows for a greater variety of perspectives informing the decision-making. It allows every topic the government touches – from federal budgets to domestic violence policies, and from environmental regulation to cultural funding – to be viewed through a multidimensional lens. It is, slowly, becoming easier to be what we can now see.

A BIG QUESTION:

Should 16- and 17-year-olds be allowed to vote?

In 2022, Aotearoa New Zealand's Supreme Court ruled that not allowing sixteen- and seventeen-year-olds to vote is in breach of the country's bill of rights, as they found it to be a form of age-based discrimination.

While no legislation has been introduced in New Zealand to change the voting age, our audience was curious as to whether the same concept could hold up in Australia.

Younger people voting is not a new idea: in 2018, the Greens introduced a bill to parliament calling for an extension of the right to vote – on an optional basis – to sixteen- and seventeen-year-olds. At the time, the Labor Party said, 'In principle, we agree . . . that sixteen- and seventeen-year-olds are as capable of participating in elections as older Australians.'

Then, in 2023, the Greens introduced a bill to bring in 'compulsory' voting for this age group, but exempting them from being fined for not voting. This time, enthusiasm from the two major parties was thin – a spokesperson for Labor told TDA it was 'not something the government is proposing' and there were 'more pressing and urgent' priorities; the Opposition spokesperson for electoral matters said it was 'certainly not one of our priorities'.

Remember, the voting age wasn't always eighteen. It was only in 1973 that the Australian Parliament amended the *Commonwealth Electoral Act 1918* to lower the minimum voting age to eighteen from twenty-one. And lowering it further is not a completely foreign idea – in fact, a small number of countries, including Argentina, Cuba, Scotland and Brazil, already allow sixteen-year-olds to vote in local, state or federal elections.

The 2022 NZ case was brought by 'Make It 16' – a group of campaigners who argued that young people should be able to vote in general elections and have their say on critical issues such as climate change, housing prices, education and mental health. The group argued that because sixteen- and seventeen-year-olds can work full-time, pay taxes and drive a car, surely they should have a say in shaping the policies that affect those spheres.

Both times the Greens have introduced the idea of younger people voting, they've centred their arguments on three core ideas:

- **RESPONSIBILITY** Sixteen-year-olds are accountable in other ways so they should have a say in the decisions that affect their lives
- **CIVIC ENGAGEMENT** To get young people to care more about politics, we should give them a vested interest in the decisions that will shape their futures
- **PARTICIPATION** By mobilising young people, we increase the chance of teenagers deciding a political career is for them, and entering the arena.

However, as with every issue, there are arguments against lowering the voting age. Common ones include maturity (that this age group lacks the life experience and judgement necessary to fully understand the implications of their votes); a lower cognitive ability to make informed political decisions; and political knowledge (younger teens won't make informed decisions because they don't have a thorough understanding of the issues they're voting on, leading to voting based on misinformation/disinformation and peer pressure).

Countering this, Tabitha Stephenson-Jones, an organiser of the 'Make It 16 Australia' campaign, said young people are 'engaged, enthusiastic and ready to make a difference, the only issue is – politicians are afraid'.

Indeed, some experts believe part of the resistance from the major parties in Australia is because they're worried about their own support base. According to a Resolve Poll from 2022, more than 40 per cent of eighteen- to thirty-four-year-olds intended not to vote for the two major parties in the federal election of that year. And there's a chance the percentage of sixteen- to eighteen-year-olds who feel the same way may be even higher.

What do you think?

THE
ECON

2.

OMY

WHY SHOULD I CARE ABOUT THE ECONOMY?

Look, we know a chapter about economics may not get your pulse racing. But even if it's not the world's most thrilling subject, the economy matters – we're all in it, whether we like it or not, and it determines so much about our lives.

We think one reason it so often seems like a boring subject is because it's basically written in a foreign language (inflation, deficits, nominal GDP).

Many of us are not taught that language. Perhaps we were taught a little financial literacy in a maths class at school. If we took commerce or business studies, we might have gone a bit further. But many of us left school without even fundamental knowledge about, say, how our tax system works.

Research shows there is a significant financial literacy gap for the typical Daily Aus reader: a survey by the ANZ bank, which rated customers on their financial knowledge, found those aged under thirty-five performed worst.[1] According to that research, it was because they had 'limited personal experience' with many financial products. In other words, young people didn't understand mortgages because most had never had one.

Unsurprisingly, we don't think you should be shut out of understanding the economy just because you're shut out of the housing market. So, let's change this lack of financial literacy.

We'll try to translate the language of economics into something that's not just digestible but might even be enjoyable! Sound like a tough sell? We reckon we can change your mind.

Let's dive in.

KNOWLEDGE IS POWER (AND MONEY)

Since 2001, the University of Melbourne has run an annual survey tracking about 17,000 Australians, asking questions about a variety of subjects.[2]

To specifically test financial literacy, the survey asks five questions about basic financial concepts.

The finding? Less than half of those surveyed could answer all five questions correctly. The result is worst for those aged under twenty-five, and concerningly there is also a gender gap (50 per cent of men scored a perfect five, while only 35 per cent of women did).

And here's where things get really worrying – the survey has also found low financial literacy can translate to poor financial health. Poverty rates are twice as high among the least financially literate compared to the most literate group. Those with low financial literacy are less likely to get involved in household budget decisions; they have a lower appetite to save; and they are more likely to experience financial stress.

There are lots of ways this link could be explained. For example, it's likely people raised in financially privileged backgrounds would have more opportunity to learn financial literacy.

But whatever the reason, these findings issue a warning – the less you know about how money works, the less money you're likely to have.

AUSTRALIA'S MONEY

What is the economy, anyway?

This seems like a sensible place to start. Here's a definition from the Reserve Bank of Australia (RBA): the economy is 'the system for deciding how scarce resources are used so that goods and services can be produced and consumed'. In other words, it's the way a society decides who gets what and how.

Usually when we think of the economy, we think of money – how to get it, how to save it, how to spend it. There's no doubt money is central to the way the economy runs. But the economy goes deeper than money. It's society's answer to fundamental questions such as, will you have enough to eat? Will you be able to put a roof over your head? What standard of living can you expect to have?

And the economy isn't some mysterious being – you *are* the economy. When you have a job, you get something out of the economy (money in your pocket), but you also put something into it (whatever you produce at work).

You contribute to the success of the economy, and you are affected by it in turn. When it's in good health, you'll feel it; it might be easier for you to find a job, for example. When the economy is struggling, you'll feel that too.

We think that's why stories about the economy always elicit such strong emotions in our readers – even if we don't always understand it as well as we'd like, we grasp how much it matters when we can't get a pay rise or keep up with our rent.

What type of economy are we?

Different countries structure their economies in different ways. To start thinking about these structures, here are two extreme scenarios.

In the first extreme, everybody is left to fend for themselves. The answer to the question of 'Who gets what and how?' is: 'You get what you can take.'

In the second extreme, every decision is made for you. The answer to 'Who gets what and how?' is: 'You get what you're given.'

Most real-world economies sit somewhere between these two extremes. Australia is no exception.

Australia is a mixed market economy. Our government provides some things centrally – usually things we consider essential for everyone, like roads, schools and hospitals. But most other things are distributed in 'markets', where we can largely buy and sell whatever we choose.

Governments still have a role to protect us from theft or exploitation in markets, but beyond that we are free: you can work for anyone who is willing to hire you and you can buy something from anyone who is willing to sell it to you.

In a market, the price of something is driven by two forces: supply and demand. Demand refers to what we're willing to pay for something, and supply refers to what businesses are willing to sell it for. The price is the balance of these two forces.

We can apply this logic to all sorts of prices. Take a phone, for example: if a popular new model comes out, it will be able to command a high price because everyone wants it. Meanwhile, the old model will get cheaper as sellers decide to get rid of it.

Let's look at a real-world example: petrol. When Russia invaded Ukraine in February 2022, much of the world responded by putting sanctions (restrictions) on Russian goods, including oil. Russia sells a lot of oil to the world, so this decision meant there was suddenly a lot less to go around, including in Australia.

Of course, the number of Australian drivers who needed petrol for their vehicles didn't change. With less petrol available, but the same number of drivers who wanted it, petrol stations in Australia raised their prices.

This might seem unfair – why should petrol stations be allowed to charge you more for something you can't go without? The short answer: it's a free market. Apart from regulations that protect you from a blatant rip-off, there's no law that stops a petrol station from charging you whatever it wants.

But if that's the case, why $2 and not $10? Well, if there was only one petrol station in the country, you might indeed be charged $10 or more. But there isn't. Individual petrol stations have to compete with one another to win your business. That competition is the 'secret sauce' of a market. A petrol station can't charge $10 because if their competitor charged $9 they'd lose all their customers. It is competition which helps to balance supply and demand and ensure the final price is 'fair'.

In a market, supply and demand shape everything, from the price of a home to plane tickets. These prices won't always seem fair – for example, in markets where there isn't much competition, businesses have enough market power to charge you more than they would if they had competitors. But thinking in terms of the market 'forces' of supply and demand is a good way to start unpicking why something costs what it does.

For now, the most important thing to remember is that, apart from essentials provided by the government, if we want to buy something we have to buy it in a market.

What does the government do?

The government has an important role to play in a mixed market economy like Australia's.

First, it provides some goods and services itself. If you want to drive from Sydney to Melbourne, you'll have to obtain a car, but the government has already built a road, which is generally free for you to use (apart from the occasional toll). Deciding what to provide and how to provide it is one of the most important economic jobs for a government.

Second, it sets the rules of the game for markets. The government passes laws against theft and establishes police and courts to enforce them. It can set product standards (e.g. food safety regulations), require honest behaviour (e.g. false advertising laws) or even ban products altogether (e.g. some recreational drugs or weapons).

Third, the government tries to maintain the overall health of an economy. When economists talk about the economy as a whole (rather than an individual market), they often call it the 'macro economy'.

How do we measure the performance of an economy?

There are many ways we can evaluate economies. How evenly are resources shared? How well is the environment being looked after? How happy are the people in a society?

But the most common starting point is simply to measure an economy's size. We do this using a number called Gross Domestic Product (GDP).

GDP is one big counting exercise – it counts all the goods and services produced within a country's borders, expressed by their monetary value.

For example, imagine if Australia only produced chocolate milk and dance lessons. Suppose choccy milk is $3 a carton, and we produce ten cartons a year. Dance lessons are $5 a lesson, and we produce twenty lessons a year. That means we're producing $30 of chocolate milk and $100 of dance lessons a year. So our GDP would be $130.

We can use this number to compare countries to one another, or to track how an economy changes over time: is it growing or is it shrinking?

In the broadest terms, if GDP is growing, an economy is doing well – think more workers in jobs, and more money in people's banks accounts (although GDP alone doesn't tell us whether the growth is shared around).

If GDP shrinks, the economy has some problems – think high unemployment and falling wages.

So, what's Australia's GDP, and how does it stack up by global standards?

Here are two lists that tell us slightly different things.

First, there's overall GDP. Top of the list are the countries we typically think of as the biggest, starting with the US and China.

Second, there's GDP per capita (per person). This tells us which country has the wealthiest people, regardless of the total size of the economy.

COUNTRIES WITH THE **HIGHEST NOMINAL GDP** IN 2023 (US$)[3]

1. **USA** — **$26.85 TRILLION**
2. **CHINA** — **$19.37 TRILLION**
3. **JAPAN** — **$4.41 TRILLION**
4. **GERMANY** — **$4.31 TRILLION**
5. **INDIA** — **$3.74 TRILLION**
13. **AUSTRALIA** — **$1.71 TRILLION**

COUNTRIES WITH THE **HIGHEST GDP PER CAPITA** IN 2023 (US$)

1. **LUXEMBOURG** — **$132,732**
2. **IRELAND** — **$114,581**
3. **NORWAY** — **$101,103**
4. **SWITZERLAND** — **$98,767**
5. **SINGAPORE** — **$91,900**
9. **AUSTRALIA** — **$64,964**

They're quite different lists, but Australia is close to the top on both.

Why care about economic growth?

We're interested in economic growth because a growing economy is often associated with better living standards.

Think of a very small economy – say, a village with cows and chickens. If one year the village suddenly has more cows and chickens producing more milk and eggs, a few things happen.

1. **Fewer villagers go hungry because there's more milk and eggs.**

2. **More villagers are employed because more workers are needed to tend to the extra animals, and these workers make more money.**

3. **The village government might collect more tax from these village workers and so it has more to pay for healthcare or education.**

Sure enough, we do see a link between economic growth and non-economic measures of wellbeing such as life expectancy. 'Advanced' economies (with higher GDP per person) tend to have more advanced standards of living.

Of course, pursuing economic growth at all costs can have other consequences we care about. Again, GDP alone tells us nothing about how a country's resources are distributed – what if one farmer keeps all the milk and eggs and the other villagers starve? GDP is an important number, but it's just one number.

How does the government manage the economy?

Now, let's turn back to one of the key players in any economy: the government.

There's no more important government document when it comes to the economy than the government's annual budget. It shapes how much tax you pay, what your university fees are, what medical treatments you can access and maybe even whether you'll be able to purchase a house. But what *is* it?

Let's start simple. Just like a household budget, the government's budget can be split into two components: how money is earned and how it is spent.

Governments can get money in two ways – by raising taxes, or by borrowing money.

MONEY COMES IN

The federal government's three biggest sources of tax are:

1. Personal income tax

2. Company tax

3. Goods and services tax (GST)

MONEY GOES OUT

What does the federal government spend that money on? Here are the top four areas of spending, or expenditure:

1. Welfare and social security (e.g. Centrelink payments, disability care, aged care)

2. Health (states and territories also fund health)

3. Education (states and territories also fund education)

4. Defence

- PERSONAL INCOME TAX
- COMPANY TAX
- GOODS AND SERVICES TAX
- DEFENCE
- MONEY FOR STATES AND TERRITORIES TO SPEND
- HEALTH
- EDUCATION
- WELFARE & SOCIAL SECURITY

In each of these areas are all sorts of small things we might care about – medicine or a university course fee, for example. But we also need to think about how *overall* levels of tax compare to overall levels of spending.

If the government raises more money than it spends in a year, we say its budget is in surplus. When a government spends more than it raises, the budget is in deficit.

Whenever there is a deficit, the government makes up the gap by borrowing money, which it agrees to pay back at some future date with interest. This is called debt. Deficits increase the amount of debt and surpluses decrease them.

DEBT IS NOT ALWAYS A DIRTY WORD

The word 'debt' has negative associations – if you borrow a lot of money and find yourself in a lot of debt that you can't repay, you'll land yourself in a fair bit of trouble, and you'll certainly struggle to find anyone willing to lend to you again.

But government budgets are not like our personal budgets. For governments, debt is an important and useful tool. Every single government in the world has some debt. We can think of it as a way to unlock more spending today than would otherwise be possible. Of course, it has a cost: the interest the government will eventually have to pay on that debt.

Is that cost worth it? The short answer is it depends what you spend it on.

If the government uses the money in ways that improve the economy, maybe by putting more people through university or building more affordable housing, the situation is like that village with its extra cows and chickens: the country gets richer, the government collects more tax, and it can afford its interest bill.

There are lots of reasons why governments will want to run deficits and accumulate debt, especially during weak economic periods.

But governments do have to be careful. If they run up too much debt, their interest bill might get very expensive. If it gets really out of control, in the worst-case scenario a government might 'default' – fail to pay back its debts. This seriously hurts its credibility and its ability to borrow more in future.

As we can see, the government is a very important player in an economy – it can use its budget to help the economy through a crisis, but abusing its budget can create a crisis of its own.

To understand this a little better, let's take a look at the two main types of 'crisis' that can commonly hit an economy, and how the government responds to each: inflation and recession.

What is inflation?

In its simplest form, inflation means prices rising – not one price, but the total 'level' of prices across an economy.

Why does this happen? To answer that, we'll need our new friends supply and demand. Inflation is typically caused by one of two things (or both!): too much demand or not enough supply.

Let's unpack that with two hypotheticals.

First, imagine if we wake up tomorrow and half the items in every supermarket have vanished. Suddenly, there's a bigger-than-usual scramble for the remaining items. The supermarket owners can get away with charging higher prices. Not enough supply = inflation.

Second, imagine if we wake up tomorrow and everyone has an extra million dollars. We'd likely all run out for a shopping spree and would be willing to pay a lot more for things than we were yesterday, since we're all flush with cash. Again, businesses can get away with higher prices. Too much demand = inflation.

Ask yourself this: is anyone richer in the second scenario? The technical answer is, yes, a million dollars richer! But the meaningful answer is, no: you have a million dollars more, but so does everyone else, so you're really no better off. Once prices go up, you won't be able to buy anything you couldn't afford before.

Inflation on its own is not necessarily a problem, and in fact a little inflation is considered healthy. But if inflation gets out of control, it can have negative consequences. When prices change rapidly and unpredictably, it's hard to make big financial decisions, and if your wages can't keep up, your cost of living will be greater.

For this reason, governments and central banks get particularly concerned about major periods of inflation. This could happen for any number of reasons. For example, inflation can be kick-started by a big global event, like a war, which suddenly cuts off access to something everyone needs. This is exactly what happened around the world in 2022 when Russia invaded Ukraine, restricting the global supply of oil, gas and wheat, and setting off inflation around the world.

FIGHTING INFLATION

Suppose inflation breaks out. What can be done?

There are a few options for government. Remember, the problem is effectively that there is too much spending (demand) and not enough to buy (supply). There's not usually much governments can do in the short term to get more supply of something that's running out, but governments can reduce demand by taking money out of the economy.

The government can do this with its own budget, by raising taxes or cutting spending. But the most common tool to fight inflation sits with the central bank: interest rates.

Interest rates

Interest is the price you pay someone for lending you money. If your friend lends you $100 today and asks for $101 back tomorrow, the extra $1 is the interest – in this case, an interest rate of 1 per cent.

You can think of this rate as paying your friend for their trouble. Alternatively, you can think of it as compensating them for the risk they took on when they parted with their $100 – the risk of you losing it and being unable to pay them back.

If your friend is willing to lend to you with just a 1 per cent interest rate, that's a sign they trust you. If, on the other hand, they ask you to pay them back $150, it'd be a sign they're worried you won't repay and are looking for some extra reassurance.

What does any of this have to do with inflation?

The RBA has the power to change the interest rate it charges banks, with the expectation banks will pass any changes on to their customers. If the RBA increases the interest rate it charges banks, and the banks increase rates for their own customers, the result is that borrowing money becomes more expensive for everyone. If it's more expensive, people are less likely to borrow. If people borrow less, they have less to spend, and there's less demand to push up inflation.

There's no getting around it – this stuff is enough to make your head hurt. But the long and the short of it is this: interest rates are an important tool for central banks to fight inflation. They are like medicine for inflation. However, it's painful medicine. It makes anyone with a mortgage, or another kind of loan, pay more, which can be very difficult for anyone on a tight budget.

The RBA is aware of this, and it has to balance its efforts to fight inflation against the risk of going too far in the other direction. If the RBA cuts spending too much, it could unleash the other type of economic natural disaster.

Drum roll, please, for the big R . . .

What is a recession?

A recession is a period of economic decline.

We can measure it using GDP – if a country's GDP shrinks for six months in a row, we say it is 'officially' in a recession.

Why do recessions happen? It can be just about anything. In the 1990s, a recession was caused because investors suddenly decided they'd become overexcited about new internet businesses and withdrew their investments. In 2008, a major worldwide recession was caused by a collapse in the US housing market. In 2020, a recession was caused by the pandemic, which saw entire cities grind to a halt and many forms of economic activity cease.

The causes might be different, but the consequences are usually the same: in a recession, spending is low, businesses are forced to shut and jobs are lost.

FIGHTING A RECESSION

Governments and central banks fight recessions by trying to encourage spending.

The government can do this via its budget by cutting taxes or raising spending. We call this stimulus. The government did this during the pandemic by giving money to businesses to pay staff who couldn't work during lockdowns, to keep businesses, people and spending afloat.

The central bank can help, too, by cutting interest rates instead of raising them so that it becomes easier to borrow and easier to spend.

Sounds like the exact opposite of an inflation crisis? You're on the money. Economists often talk about the economy as moving in a cycle – periods of recession and stimulus are often followed by periods of out-of-control spending and inflation. Rinse, repeat.

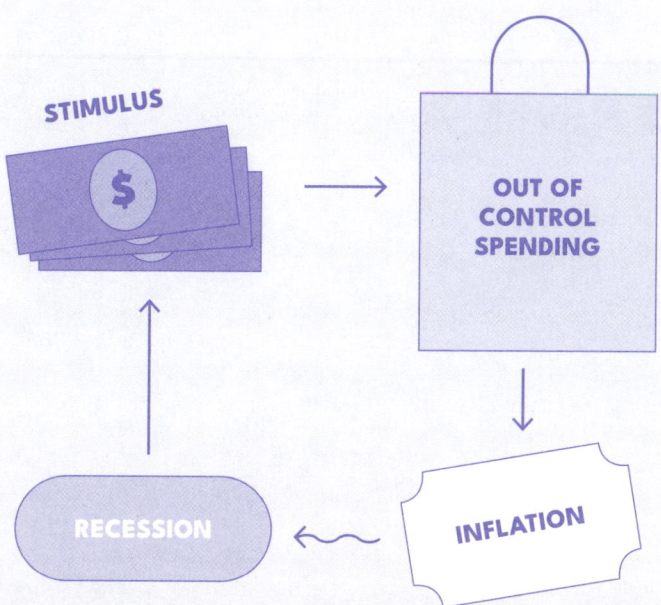

The economy is a mysterious being the economy. W have a job, you out of the econ your pocket) bu something into you produce at

t some
– you are
en you
t something
y (money in
you also put
(whatever
ork).

DANCE BREAK:

THE FOUR-DAY WORK WEEK

Let's freshen up and change the pace. Ever wished you could work a four-day week? So have we!

Turns out the idea is becoming a reality for some, and not such a pipe dream for lots of us. In 2021, twenty organisations in Australia and Aotearoa New Zealand participated in a six-month four-day work week trial.[4] The expectation was that employees in the trial would maintain 100 per cent of their productivity while working 80 per cent of their usual week and receiving no loss of pay. The study measured staff satisfaction, retention and productivity. When we were covering this trial for a story on TDA, we spoke to a bunch of young people who were in the midst of the experiment. One, Dylan, remarked:

> 'Productivity has actually gone up. Everybody is coming back to the office much more energised.'

These sorts of trials are being rolled out globally, not just in Australia. So, what do you think? Would you be up for it?

YOUR MONEY

Anyway, let's stop dreaming of work-free Fridays and keep going. You're doing really well – and hopefully you've got a bit of a sense now of how things play out in in the broad context of The Economy.

So now let's look at the stuff that *you* really feel in *your* pocket.

We've made a list of three key components you'll need to understand about your money within the economy. If you can get your head around these ideas, you're flying:

- **Taxes**
- **Superannuation**
- **The share (or stock) market**

Taxes

Ugh, taxes! And yet taxes, and us paying them, benefit every single person in an economy, in a country. We need the money taxes raise to build schools and hospitals, fund government programs (like the unemployment payment or disability support), operate an army to defend us – the list goes on.

Any federal government money (or revenue) that doesn't come from borrowing money comes from taxes. The federal government's three main revenue sources are: personal income tax, company tax, and goods and services tax (GST). Let's dive in to each one.

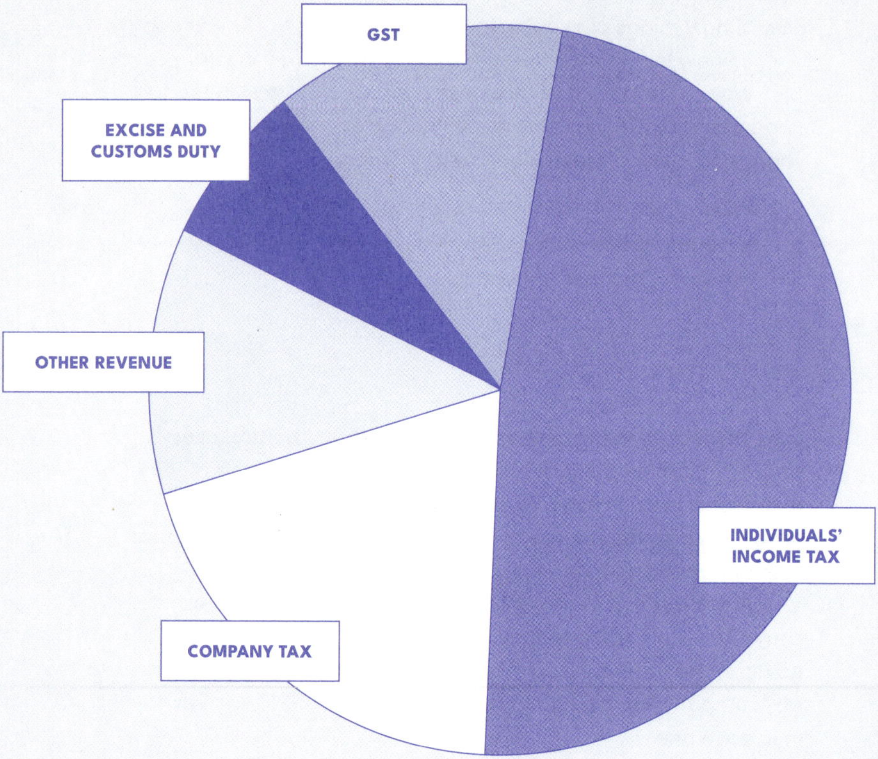

SOURCES OF AUSTRALIAN FEDERAL GOVERNMENT REVENUE

- GST
- EXCISE AND CUSTOMS DUTY
- OTHER REVENUE
- INDIVIDUALS' INCOME TAX
- COMPANY TAX

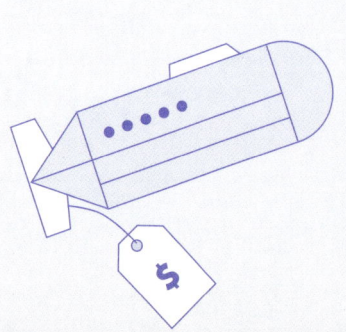

THE ECONOMY

PERSONAL INCOME TAX

WHAT Personal income tax is the tax you pay on any income you earn.

RATE The more you earn, the more tax you pay. As of 2023, if you earn less than $18,200, you don't pay any tax. After that, the amount you pay steadily increases, starting at 15 cents for every dollar and ending with 45 cents of every dollar you earn above $180,000.

How do you pay? If you're on a payroll, the tax is usually taken out of your salary automatically. If you're self-employed, you need to set aside enough to pay what you owe the Australian Tax Office (ATO) yourself.

Then, at the end of each financial year, it's 'tax time' – you'll have to fill out a form called a  tax return to make sure you've paid the right amount.

Your tax return is where you can claim back some of the tax you've paid if you bought anything that was tax-exempt during the year. For example, you don't have to pay tax on most work-related expenses, so you might be able to claim a little back for these. Just make sure you keep your receipts!

THE STAT

50% — The percentage of all federal government revenue that comes from personal income tax

---

COMPANY TAX

23 per cent of all federal government revenue comes from company tax.

WHAT This is the tax companies pay on their profits. When companies don't make a profit, they don't pay tax.

RATE For big companies, 30 per cent. For businesses classified as small, 27.5 per cent. But you'll rarely see big companies paying the full 30 per cent.

WAIT, SO WHY DO SOME COMPANIES NOT PAY TAX?

There's a narrative you read often in the news that the big multinational companies (and even some Australian companies) don't pay any, or enough, tax. How does that even happen?

The devil is in the detail! Just like for personal income tax, company tax has lots of exceptions and 'loopholes' that can change how much tax you have to pay. This opens up avenues for a bit of accounting trickery. The three main ways companies use the rules to minimise their tax bill are by:

1. CLAIMING A LOSS

2. USING TAX CONCESSIONS/DEDUCTIONS

3. 'SHIFTING' REVENUE TO ANOTHER COUNTRY

BUSINESS LOSSES If your business loses money one year, your profits will be zero and you won't have to pay any tax for that year. But you're allowed to carry forward that loss and subtract it from a future year when you do make a profit. Businesses can spread out their losses in this way to reduce the total amount of tax they pay.

CONCESSIONS/DEDUCTIONS If businesses commit to certain activities, they get tax discounts, which are known as concessions or deductions. For example, businesses get a concession for some types of research and development spending. Some companies try to take advantage of deductions, and in 2021 the Greens suggested a policy to clamp down on these kinds of concessions.

SCAN ME FOR MORE

OFFSHORE COMPANIES If you're a multinational company (think Apple or Google), in which country do you pay your taxes? It's a question the world hasn't fully resolved. Here's one rule you could use: if you make money in a country, you should pay tax on that money according to the rules in that country. Simple, right? Unfortunately, that's not the current reality. Multinationals often use complicated arrangements to ensure they pay tax only in countries with generous tax laws. Governments across the world are working together to change these rules, but progress has been slow.

GOODS AND SERVICES TAX (GST)

One tax no company can avoid is goods and services tax. GST is a 10 per cent charge on most goods and services, which gets added to the purchase price. (It is estimated that 160 countries have a tax equivalent of GST, but the percentage of tax varies depending on the country.)

GST has been a divisive political topic in Australia over the years since it was introduced. The Coalition floated the idea in 1991 and used it as a core strand of their 1993 election campaign. When John Howard became leader of the Liberal Party in 1995 he said he would 'never, ever' introduce GST. However, after becoming prime minister in 1996 he passed the tax reforms after negotiating a number of amendments and changes.

GST now comprises 14 per cent of all federal government revenue.

WHAT Since 2000, GST has been applied to almost everything you've bought. So, if you buy a $110 TV, $10 will have gone to the government. That's GST.

RATE As mentioned, 10 per cent of the good or service. But it's worth noting the GST isn't applied to absolutely everything – more on this below.

GST is paid by consumers (customers) on most goods and services. The business then passes the taxed amount (e.g. $10 for that TV) on to the federal government. The funds are then distributed by the federal government to the states and territories to support their own budgets.

Some items and necessities are exempt from GST. They include:

- **fresh food (e.g. meat, fish, fruit, veg, flour)**
- **some education costs (including private school fees)**
- **some medical and health costs and goods (including menstrual products)**
- **some religious services and charitable activities**
- **water, sewerage and drainage**

WHY IS THE GST CONTROVERSIAL?

Those who oppose the GST point out that it places a bigger burden on people with lower incomes. Everybody pays $10 GST on that same television, but that $10 represents a much larger share of a low income than a high income. That is a different principle to how we structure income tax, where people with higher incomes pay a greater share of their incomes as tax.

On the other hand, some people prefer GST to income or company taxes because it's harder to avoid and it's consistently applied – 10 per cent for (almost) everything.[5]

Superannuation

Superannuation (or 'super') is money that is taken out of your pay and put into a 'fund', which is set aside for your retirement. In most cases, you won't be able to access this money until you're at least sixty, if at that point you have retired.

Since the 1990s, the government has required by law that every employer puts a certain percentage of each of their employees' pay into super (known as the 'superannuation guarantee' or compulsory support). As of July 2023, that amount is 11 per cent, but it will reach 12 per cent by 2025. Employees can choose to contribute more than this if they wish and there are government incentives to do so.

What happens to the money? It gets invested, and (hopefully) makes a return. Because the money stays in for years, it can increase by surprising amounts. If you put in $10,000 into a super fund at the age of twenty and it grows by a modest 5 per cent a year, then you take it out fifty years later, it will be worth more than $100,000. Yes, ten times more!

Of course, this all depends on whether your money is invested well and makes a consistent return. You can choose to manage your super fund yourself, but most people put their money in dedicated super funds where it's is invested alongside the money of many others.

The role of a super fund is to carefully choose how your money is invested. Saving for retirement is a marathon, not a sprint, so super fund managers try to find investments to allow money to grow over a long period of time. Super fund managers can invest in almost anything – cryptocurrency, property and shares, even infrastructure like airports.

The share market

All this talk about investing and returns might have you thinking about the share market. Unless you live under a rock, chances are you've been bombarded with advice before investing your money in shares. But what if you're stuck at step one, with little real idea what the share market (also known as the stock market) even is?

Let's clear up a fundamental confusion before we start. The share market and the stock market are the same thing: 'share market' is the Australian term, 'stock market' is the American term. They're interchangeable. Promise.

WHAT IS A SHARE?

It's a single unit of ownership in a company or financial asset. One share = a proportion of a company, meaning if you buy a share of a company, you technically own a tiny part of that company. That single unit has a value, depending on the company's value and success. The more successful the company, the higher the price of the share.

WHAT IS THE SHARE MARKET?

This is where you buy and sell your shares (it's also known as an exchange). In Australia, the primary exchange is called the Australian Securities Exchange (ASX).

The share market is not one specific website someone can go to, and investors can't buy shares directly from 'the share market'. Individual investors need what is known as a 'broker'. Think of a broker as a middle person or service that conducts the transaction between the investor (you) and the exchange (the share market). The broker completes the transaction and charges a fee to do so.

Many individual investors use an online brokerage system operated by one of the big banks, but if you're making big trades, you can get a professional broker to do the deals for you.

WHY DO PEOPLE TRADE?

Investors (people who buy shares) aim to buy shares in order to eventually sell them at (hopefully) a higher price, with the goal of making a profit.

Owning shares is also a way to diversify your wealth and have different streams of income. People can make quite a lot of money from the share market with the right knowledge and good investment strategies.

But what goes up can also come down: when share prices go down, as an investor you can lose money. That's why educating yourself about which companies and industry sectors you invest in is super important.

WHY DO THE PRICES OF SHARES CHANGE?

The prices change for numerous reasons, but it's usually due to new information about the company. Anything from new earnings (how much the company has made in the past quarter or year) to the business changing strategic direction, sentiment (how people are feeling about a company or its leadership), world news (when there's global conflict, people begin to doubt there are strong economic times ahead), political leadership changes (a new leader in a country could have different visions around corporate tax, innovation or competition), to people of public interest tweeting about a company (it used to be that if Elon Musk praised a company as a good investment, the stock in that company rose) – these can all have an impact on the price of the share.

Why? You know this! It's our old friend supply and demand – the more people who want to purchase shares in a company, the higher the price goes.

> If you've made it this far, congratulations! You're well on your way to being an economic and financial whiz. Let's take a walk on the bright side now.

THE BRIGHT SIDE

We've all heard the adage 'money buys you happiness'. But what happens if we flip it? Can happiness make you money? Are there economic benefits from being happy? What happens to our economy when we are more optimistic?

There's been a surprising amount of research into the link between positivity and economic growth over decades. Within each study there are nuances and complexities we can't capture here, but what we do know is that it's only since the late 1990s and early 2000s that economists and psychologists have firmed up a link between happy societies and economic prosperity. That said, it's important to remember that we're just talking about the most likely scenarios. There are plenty of happy people who don't make much money, and plenty of wealthy people who are pretty miserable.

So, what's the take-home message of the research? Being happy makes you more likely to earn more money.

In 1995, Carol Graham of the Brookings Institution tracked the happiness and wealth of a group of Russians over five years. This is called a 'longitudinal study' and is an effective way for researchers to measure change over time.

By the time Graham checked in with the same group in 2000, she found the happier people had higher incomes than the less happy ones, and were more likely to be in good health.[6]

But, wait. How do we know that being happy made these people earn more, and not that higher wages led to their greater levels of happiness? The researchers acknowledged this, and identified something they described as 'unexplained happiness'. This was happiness that couldn't be drawn to pre-existing attributes; for example, if someone recently married, had a child . . . or got a high-paying job. It was among these individuals that researchers could draw a line between happiness *before* they started to earn money and their higher wages *after* they joined the workforce. They found that one 'point' of intrinsic happiness in 1995 led to about a 3 per cent higher income in 2000.[7]

And the elements of happiness that had the most impact on earning? Optimism and self-esteem.

Here in Australia, researchers have been busy asking the same questions, and finding similar results. Remember that University of Melbourne survey we talked about at the beginning of the chapter? Well, economists at the University of Western Sydney used its data to look at whether happy people earnt more. They found an individual who is satisfied with their life earns $1766.70 a year more than someone who is unsatisfied with life. For every one-percentage-point increase in someone's happiness, there was an increase in the person's income of 0.05 per cent.[8]

Of course, happiness is relative. There are questions of how to measure it (the answers to surveys can fluctuate based on how the survey-taker is feeling that day); about cultural nuances in how we express happiness (in some countries, expressing happiness could be tied up with gloating and a failure to exhibit modesty); and the environmental factors that can skew results (people in countries with different models of universal healthcare and education, such as some northern European nations, tend to be happier regardless of individual wealth because everyone enjoys the benefit of being part of a wealthy society).

Happier people, according to Australian research, tend to be more active, more productive, and get less upset by their work. And that must be good for the economy!

A BIG QUESTION:

Let's start at the beginning. HECS stands for Higher Education Contribution Scheme. Most Australian university students have to pay for some or all of their degree. However, Australia allows students to defer payment by offering them an 'income-contingent' loan – that's a loan from the government that you only have to pay back if you earn more than a certain amount.

This loan is usually called HECS-HELP or FEE-HELP, depending on your course type. (HELP stands for Higher Education Loan Program.) There are similar loans for some Vocational Education and Training (VET) courses (called VET Study Loans or VSL).

You only have to repay your loan when you earn more than a certain amount (currently $48,361 per annum). When your income is higher than this threshold, you must pay a set percentage of your income. That percentage is higher for those with higher income – for example, somebody earning $75k must pay 4.5 per cent of their income, and someone earning $100k must pay 7 per cent. Typically, your employer will take this percentage out of your pay cheque automatically. At tax time, the ATO will figure out if you have overpaid or underpaid what you owe for the financial year and make any corrections.

The government does not charge interest on your loan and any outstanding debt is forgiven when you die. However, there is one catch that you need to remember: the loans get indexed.

Indexation is an update to the dollar amount of your loan to reflect the present day's prices. Why is that? Because the value of a dollar changes over time – think of grocery items that once cost a few cents but now cost several dollars, not because they are necessarily more expensive but because a dollar counts for less.

The government updates the dollar amount of many of its loans and payments regularly to preserve their 'real' value. They also do this for welfare payments.

That indexation can be particularly painful for those with loans when prices are rising fast. In May 2023, the Australian Tax Office confirmed student loans would be increased by 7.1 per cent from the following month. The large increase reflected high inflation at the time.

So, what can you do in these situations? Well, you can choose to pay back more of your loan on top of the standard percentage at any time, if you wish. You can also apply to the Australian Tax Office (ATO) to defer repayment on financial hardship grounds. We can't give you any financial advice in this book (or anywhere!), so the question of whether early repayment is beneficial really depends on your unique financial situation.

OUR
CLIM

3.

IATE

WHY SHOULD I CARE ABOUT CLIMATE CHANGE?

To understand why you should care about climate change, you first need to understand what we mean when we discuss 'climate change'. Climate change refers to a shift in temperatures and weather patterns over time. Crucially, its key driver has been found to be human activities, specifically the burning of fossil fuels.

Before we get into the nuts and bolts of climate change policy, it's worth taking a second to unpack some of the basic terminology.

Since scientists first started monitoring the amount of carbon dioxide (CO_2) in the atmosphere in the late 1950s, they have noticed a trend. The more carbon we pump into the atmosphere, the warmer the surface temperature on Earth gets. As a result of human activities, particularly those that pump out heat-trapping greenhouse gases, the Earth is now at least 1.1 degrees Celsius warmer than it was between 1850 and 1900. Most of the warming has happened since 1975, and the past two decades have been the warmest since record-keeping of temperature began in 1880.[1]

Today, there is a 95 per cent chance that by the end of this century the Earth will have warmed by up to 2 degrees Celsius above late-1800s levels.

We get it – one or two degrees may not sound like a lot. But the climate is a fragile system. Scientists warn that 2 degrees of warming could cause significant damage and make parts of the world uninhabitable. Satellite images from space show that Arctic sea ice is decreasing rapidly, and glaciers are disappearing around the world. Sea levels are rising, and humidity is increasing too.

So why should you care? The impacts of climate change won't just be felt in one part of the world. The warming of the globe affects everybody – and everything – on this planet. Understanding what is contributing to it – and what can stop it – is fundamental to navigating the modern world.

KEY TERMS YOU WILL READ ABOUT IN CLIMATE NEWS

FOSSIL FUELS The three main fossil fuels are coal, crude oil and natural gas. Fossil fuels are extracted from the Earth through mining and drilling and are then burnt for energy purposes such as heat production (think: gas cooking, water heaters), powering engines (as in our cars, trains and planes) or generating electricity. Burning fossil fuels produces (or emits) carbon dioxide, which is a greenhouse gas. The supply of fossil fuels is finite – eventually, inevitably, they will run out.

EMISSIONS There are two types of emissions that impact the environment. First, there are emissions that pollute the air we breathe – such as nitrogen dioxide and carbon monoxide. They are unhealthy for living things (think of 'dirty air' in a big city). Second, there are greenhouse gas emissions, which have a long-term effect on climate rather than air quality. These are the emissions we're mostly talking about in this chapter. We will often refer to them as 'carbon emissions', referring to carbon dioxide, the most significant greenhouse gas emitted as a result of human activity.

GREENHOUSE GAS A gas that behaves like a 'greenhouse' when it builds up in the atmosphere – it traps in heat, which in large quantities can warm the planet and damage the environment. The most abundant greenhouse gases in the Earth's atmosphere are carbon dioxide, methane, water vapour, ozone and nitrous oxide. Burning fossil fuels is the main way humans add greenhouse gas to the atmosphere (specifically carbon dioxide). Clearing land and forests also emits carbon dioxide, as the carbon stored within soil and trees is released into the atmosphere.

So here's the state of play. According to a climate report released by the UN Intergovernmental Panel on Climate Change (IPCC) in March 2023, human activity has 'unequivocally' caused average temperatures to warm. As we outlined before, this warming has already had 'widespread' adverse effects, including extinctions, extreme weather events, glacial melting and food insecurity. And we already know the effects have generally been worse for those in low-income countries. Looking forward, higher warming is raising the likelihood of 'irreversible' damage – events like mass extinctions or the melting of glaciers, which cannot be reversed even if we eventually use 'cooling' techniques to lower global temperatures again.

So how did we get here?

A BRIEF HISTORY

For more than thirty years, global leaders have known about our warming planet. At global summits, they have negotiated, set targets, made promises, negotiated some more, laid out pledges, set new targets and so on.

The IPCC was set up by the United Nations in 1988 and produced its first scientific report in 1990. The goal of the IPCC was to make sure that global leaders were always in touch with the best and most up-to-date science on climate change. Two years after that report, the United Nations, with support from governments around the world, held an Earth Summit in Rio de Janeiro, Brazil.

A TIMELINE OF GLOBAL CLIMATE SUMMITS

1992
RIO

Rio was a wake-up moment – or, at least, it seemed like one. Presented with powerful evidence of the existence of climate change, world leaders decided to take action. Among other things, Rio gave us four conventions: the United Nations Framework Convention on Climate Change (UNFCCC), the Rio Declaration, the Convention on Biological Diversity and the Declaration on the Principles of Forest Management. The most significant of these was the UNFCCC. It bound member states to act in the interests of human safety even in the face of scientific uncertainty, and set out specific goals for how countries would address climate change. At the same time, the UNFCCC recognised that while all countries should have a common goal, they might need different routes to get there. After all, developed countries like the US and Australia had produced far more emissions since industrialisation than smaller, less developed economies.

1997
KYOTO

The UNFCCC sounded great on paper – but how were the countries that had signed it going to hold each other to account and meet the convention's objectives?

Well, they meet annually at the 'Conference of the Parties' (COP) to check in, report their national emission inventories and move negotiations forward. At the third COP, referred to as COP3, in Kyoto, Japan, the countries used the UNFCCC as the basis for the Kyoto Protocol, a legal treaty that was signed by most of the world's countries.

Importantly, the Kyoto Protocol did not include reduction targets for developing countries, in recognition that the burden of emissions reduction should fall on developed countries that have the economic foundations to cope with the move away from fossil fuels.

One of the tricky things about these international agreements is that countries can sign on to an agreement, but nobody can enforce its protocols due to each state's sovereignty. It's a bit like a New Year's resolution. You tell yourself and everybody around you, *I swear, this is the year I'm going to get fit*, knowing full well that, because you're in charge of your own goal, nobody can make you follow through but yourself.

In 1997, three years after the UNFCCC had come into force, developed countries hadn't really done anything to reduce their emissions. Australia only made the Kyoto treaty legally binding in December 2007, almost three years after it entered into force. At the time of writing, the United States has still not ratified Kyoto.

2009
COPENHAGEN

There was a lot riding on COP15, taking place in Copenhagen, Denmark, in 2009, but in the end, the summit only produced a political statement reiterating that it was important to limit global warming to no more than 2 degrees Celsius above pre-industrial levels. There were no concrete commitments made by attendee nations on practical ways to limit warming, with developed countries refusing to adopt specific emissions reduction targets. The summit ended without a binding global agreement or a timetable for creating one.

2015
PARIS

The Paris Agreement that arose out of COP21 had more support from individual nations than any previous agreement, and its goal was clear: limit global warming to well below 2 degrees Celsius – preferably 1.5 degrees – compared to pre-industrial levels. The agreement also committed signatories to something called 'climate financing', which meant providing financial support for developing nations to help them mitigate the impacts of climate change.

Paris, France

2021
GLASGOW

Attendees at the COP26 summit agreed on the Glasgow Climate Pact, which set the global agenda for action on climate change for the next decade. The pact included:

- a plan for countries to meet in 2023 to commit to further cuts to their carbon dioxide emissions

- an agreement to 'phase down' coal use (an earlier draft had the stronger phrasing 'phase out', but this was changed at the last minute to ensure the agreement could still pass)

- increased climate financing to assist developing nations in mitigating the effects of climate change and moving away from fossil fuel dependency.

HOW DO GOVERNMENTS PLAN TO REDUCE THEIR EMISSIONS?

Governments around the world have a range of policy tools available to them when it comes to responding to climate change, using legislation to restrict particular behaviours and providing funding to increase innovation and the search for greener solutions.

They can set carbon emissions targets and renewable energy targets; they can tax businesses that have a large emissions footprint; they can impose tariffs on carbon-heavy imports, and more.

What is 'net zero'?

Let's take a closer look at one of those options – setting carbon emissions targets. In the news, we hear all the time about countries setting targets, including 'net zero' targets. So what the hell is net zero?

Let's start by thinking of a bathtub.

If we plug the drain and turn on the taps, the tub will fill up. Now, imagine that those taps are very difficult to turn off – eventually we'd be faced with an overflowing tub. To avoid flooding the bathroom, we must first reduce the flow from the taps as much as possible. But, eventually, we will also need to pull out the plug to drain some of the water from the tub.

Once the output of water down the drain matches the input of water from the taps, we have net zero.

The important word here? 'Net' – meaning overall. Reaching net zero emissions doesn't necessarily mean not emitting any carbon dioxide, it just means balancing it out so that we are taking out as much as we put in. If Australia reaches net zero emissions, this means we've balanced the greenhouse gas emissions being produced and the greenhouse gas emissions taken out of the atmosphere (for example by planting more trees, which store carbon dioxide), and our bathtub isn't overflowing.

Remember, not all countries have the same emissions reduction targets. While the overarching aim of producing less greenhouse gases is consistent, each country has its own means, pace and interim goals, which are determined by a variety of factors.

The reality is that the richest countries in the world are also the ones most responsible for pumping greenhouse gases into the atmosphere due to industry and the lifestyle of the people who live

there. In fact, the emissions of the richest 1 per cent of the global population account for more than twice the combined share of the poorest 50 per cent of people.[2] Some experts argue it is unfair to impose emissions reduction targets on developing countries, which would stifle their economies and stop their people from accessing the same economic and lifestyle advantages enjoyed by many people in developed countries.

However, the debate is complicated by the fact that many of the world's biggest emitters are developing or recently developed countries, including China, India, Brazil and Indonesia. The argument over who should 'take the lead' on reducing emissions is one of the key reasons global climate action has been slow.

The emission
richest 1 per
of the global
account for m
twice the cor
share of the p
50 per cent o

of the
cent
opulation
ore than
bined
oorest
people.

OCEANS AND THE CLIMATE CRISIS

The ocean is an important element of Australia's identity: the Pacific Ocean is a defining characteristic of our region and Australia is home to one of the seven wonders of the natural world, the Great Barrier Reef.

The health of the Pacific, and of all the world's oceans, is critically important because they play a crucial role in absorbing heat from greenhouse gas emissions. Oceans absorb 90 per cent of the heat generated by emissions, according to UN Climate Change, and this is leading to ice melts, rising sea levels and marine heatwaves, which are damaging marine biodiversity. Warming waters are endangering the health of the Great Barrier Reef, reefs all round the world and more than a thousand species of marine life.

According to the International Union for Conservation of Nature, more than 1550 marine animals and plants were at risk of extinction as of the end of 2022, with climate change impacting at least 41 per cent of threatened marine species.[3] UNESCO states that more than half the world's marine species could be near extinction by 2100.

As the World Economic Forum emphasised in 2023, we 'need to protect our oceans – the planet's greatest carbon sink – or we risk losing the range of benefits they provide us with, from breathable air to the future of food supplies.'[4]

Emissions reduction: the world's report card

LEADING THE WAY

Suriname, in South America, and Bhutan, in the Himalayas, have already reached net zero. It's significantly easier to achieve this in a country where the economy isn't so reliant on sectors like steel, aluminium and gas extraction.

Finland has pledged to reach net zero by 2035, and Austria and Iceland are due to follow in 2040.

Germany and Sweden are aiming to achieve net zero by 2045. Both countries have enshrined their net zero targets in law.

MIDDLE OF THE PACK

Key Australian allies such as the UK, the US, Japan and Canada have all pledged to reach net zero by 2050.

In 2021, the Australian government committed to net zero by 2050.

Despite this commitment, some experts argue Australia is further behind its allies due to its short-term emissions reduction targets. Following the change of government in 2022, Australia's short-term, legally enshrined target is to lower emissions by 43 per cent on 2005 levels by 2030.

FALLING BEHIND

China, India, Saudi Arabia and Russia are all heavy emitters, and none of them has committed to reach net zero by 2050.

China has committed to being carbon neutral by 2060.

Indian prime minister Narendra Modi told COP26 the country had committed to a 2070 target.

Saudi Arabia and Russia have set a net zero by 2060 target.

You might be wondering why Australia finds itself in the middle of the pack here. Well, much of the country's wealth comes from the mining of natural resources. Australia is one of the three biggest exporters of coal in the world (alongside Russia and Indonesia). But our emissions reduction targets do not count emissions from any coal we export, which instead get counted in the country that buys the coal. It is our second-highest export after iron ore. We're also heavily reliant on coal domestically; it accounted for 51 per cent of total electricity generation in 2021.[5]

Australia has been relatively slow to plan its transition away from fossil fuels and towards more renewable sources. Still, renewables are coming. So how do they work, and where is Australia up to?

HELLO, RENEWABLE ENERGY

Renewable energy is produced through natural resources that are constantly replaced and never run out. This includes solar, which absorbs sunlight and converts its energy into electricity, and wind and hydro power, which convert the kinetic energy of moving water or air into electricity. Electricity storage and distribution technologies such as batteries are also broadly included under the 'renewables' heading because they can help to keep renewably generated power until we need it (for example, to store solar power generated in summer for use in winter).

Where is Australia at with renewable energy?

In 2021, Australia's total electricity generation was 29 per cent renewable – up 5 percentage points from the previous year.

Can we run Australia on 100 per cent renewable energy? It was once thought to be impossible – but studies have shown that powering the nation purely by renewable energy sources *is* possible with today's technology.[6]

So why hasn't this been done yet?

Basically, because changing the system behind Australia's energy market is *hard*. If you're reading this in New South Wales, Victoria, Queensland, South Australia, Tasmania or the ACT, then your electricity is regulated and controlled by something called the National Electricity Market, or NEM. (Western Australia and the Northern Territory have their own separate systems.)

The NEM is an incredibly large network of electricity grids that transmit energy between each other. It was created in the mid-1990s with a clear objective: to provide Australians with cheap, reliable and secure electricity. Even when it was being designed, experts predicted that embedding such large and deeply rooted infrastructure would make it difficult for renewable energy sources to compete with carbon-intensive ones.

Moving away from fossil fuels is more than just a technical problem – it requires decisions to be made by the government of the day. Our political representatives know the stakes are high with whatever policy they support – we've even seen political leaders (such as Liberal prime minister Malcolm Turnbull in 2018) be overthrown because of differing views within their own parties on these policies.

For the foreseeable future, we'll be talking about renewable energy in the same breath as non-renewable energy – it's a transition that will take time.

While there is a long way to go, the rate of installation of wind and solar electricity in Australia has been remarkable. Approximately 30 per cent of suitable dwellings in Australia have solar rooftops, a higher percentage than anywhere else in the world.[7]

EPIC COMEBACKS TO USE IN A DEBATE ABOUT THE CLIMATE

> There's no point doing anything about climate change because Australia is so small, it'll make no difference.

YOU
Well, Australia's emissions are indeed 1.3 per cent of the global total – a relatively small percentage. But Australia is only home to 0.3 per cent of the world's population. So, we're punching way above our weight per capita, and not in a good way. You also need to remember we produce a lot of coal that is then exported and counts towards other countries' emissions.

In terms of Australia's influence, you could look at it from an economic standpoint instead. We're one of the wealthiest economies in the world, with a huge amount of natural resources. There are a lot of easy wins on the table for lowering our emissions – like whole stretches of desert that could be used for solar energy – that other countries would love to have at their disposal.

If that doesn't convince you, think about sport! Australia loves outperforming our global opponents in sporting competitions – and in that context, we use the fact that we're a small nation as a badge of honour. We have no right to win as many medals as we do at the Olympics – but we often lead the pack. Why shouldn't we do the same when it comes to beating climate change?

> The climate has always changed. It's a cycle.

YOU
You're right – the climate has always changed, and will continue to change. What scientists are concerned about is the speed at which it's changing now. There's more confidence than ever that the warming of the climate since around the 1950s is caused primarily by human activity. The years since 2015 were the hottest on record.

Ultimately, we can't explain the rapid climate change by natural cycles of warming, cooling, ice ages or natural evolution. If those factors were the primary causes of climate change, it would be a process observable over a few thousand years – not a few decades.

> Extreme heat, raging bushfires, devastating drought – that's just 'Straya. Nothing to do with climate change!

YOU
Climate change isn't just causing significant, rapid increases in global average temperatures. Climate change is changing our weather systems altogether, making extreme weather worse around the world.

In Australia, we're already seeing this. Our bushfire season has continued to grow longer over the past four decades, and now lasts for 130 days a year – almost a month longer than it was in the late 1970s.[8] The modelling shows that 1.5 degrees Celsius of warming will add nine further days to the fire season in some parts of Australia.[9]

> Renewable energy is more expensive than coal.

YOU
Nope! Wind power, for example, costs about half as much as energy produced by a new coal plant, according to analysis by Bloomberg.[10] There *is* a cost associated with setting up new technologies, but another report, by the International Renewable Energy Agency, found that 62 per cent of new renewable energy projects will be cheaper than the cheapest new coal plants.[11] So, why would you build a new coal plant instead of a wind or solar farm?

The cost of renewables is also falling every year. The cost of electricity generated by solar came down by 85 per cent over the 2010s, while electricity generated by wind is down by more than 50 per cent. As technology gets more sophisticated, and as more people use clean energy, these costs will come down.

WHO *ACTUALLY* HAS POWER TO MAKE RULINGS ON CLIMATE CHANGE?

As climate change becomes a key driver of decision-making in political, social and economic contexts, it's also being considered by courts around the world.

Let's start at the top. In 2021, the United Nations Human Rights Council passed a resolution recognising that access to a safe, clean, healthy and sustainable environment is a human right. While the resolution is not legally binding, it could play a role in shaping global standards. It was under this rule that five young Australians lodged a human rights complaint with the UN in 2021, alleging that the federal government's 2030 emissions target failed to uphold the rights of young people in Australia to have access to a clean environment.

Meanwhile, in the Australian court system, eight Australian high-school students argued that the federal environment minister had a duty of care not to cause them harm resulting from climate change.

In Australia's common law system, the concept of a 'duty of care' is relatively common. When you drive a car, you owe a duty of care to your passengers and to pedestrians. Doctors owe a duty of care to their patients. In this case, the courts had to decide whether a government owed a duty of care to young people for the future state of their planet. Big question.

Seventeen-year-old Ava Princi, one of the students, said, 'This case was about young people stepping up and demanding more from the adults whose actions are determining our future wellbeing.'[12]

The students alleged that when the environment minister approved a major extension to a coal mine in northern New South Wales, it breached the minister's duty of care to young people.

The students were led by sixteen-year-old Melburnian Anjali Sharma and supported by eighty-six-year-old nun and former teacher Sister Brigid Arthur, who volunteered to be their litigation guardian. (You cannot bring a case to the Federal Court if you are under eighteen without a legal guardian.) At the time, Federal Court Justice Mordecai Bromberg found in favour of the students, saying:

> Perhaps the most startling of the potential harms demonstrated by the evidence before the court, is that one million of today's Australian children are expected to suffer at least one heat-stress episode serious enough to require acute care in a hospital. Many thousands will suffer premature death from heat stress or bushfire smoke.[13]

'This case was about young people stepping up and demanding more from the adults whose actions are determining our future wellbeing.'

Ava Princi

The environment minister at the time, Sussan Ley, appealed the court's decision, and, in March 2022, the full bench of the Federal Court ruled in her favour, finding that the environment minister *does not* have a duty of care to protect children from climate change. Despite the ruling, the students vowed to keep fighting, with Sharma saying outside the court, 'it will not deter us in our fight for a safe future'.

And it's not just individuals using the courts to take action. Vanuatu is seeking an opinion (which means they are looking for a ruling, but not necessarily on a specific situation) on climate change from the International Court of Justice, regarding the rights of present and future generations facing the impacts of climate change. In a statement, Vanuatu's government said it 'recognises that current levels of action and support for vulnerable developing countries within multilateral mechanisms are insufficient'. Vanuatu is currently facing rising sea levels and increasing frequency and severity of storms.

The International Court of Justice has not yet delivered its advisory opinion, and while the opinions of this court are not binding, they remain symbolically and morally significant, and can inform the development of international law.

Prior to the COP26 summit in 2021, Vanuatu announced it would 'drastically expand its diplomacy and advocacy', forming a coalition with other Pacific Islands and vulnerable nations.

THE YOUTH ARE TAKING CHARGE

It's only natural that you may be feeling anxious about climate change. The gravity of the challenges we face is enormous.

António Guterres, secretary-general of the United Nations, admitted in 2019: 'My generation has failed to respond properly to the dramatic challenge of climate change. This is deeply felt by young people. No wonder they are angry.' Guterres was speaking in the wake of the 2019 school strikes for climate – some of the largest student strikes in history.

You probably know the backstory to the school strikes for climate. The movement was started by Swedish student Greta Thunberg, whose goal was clear: to hold her government accountable for its promises under the Paris Agreement. It wasn't long before Thunberg's 'FridaysForFuture' concept went viral. What started with a lone student grew to involve hundreds of thousands, and soon millions of young people.

#FridaysForFuture

While climate strikes have been happening on a weekly basis since 2018, the most historic global events took place in September 2019 – dubbed the 'Global Week of Climate Action'. Around the world, approximately six million people participated in these events. Prior to the global strikes, 150 student organisers from around the world issued an open letter in the *Guardian*:

'We, the young, are deeply concerned about our future . . . We are the voiceless future of humanity. We will no longer accept this injustice . . . We finally need to treat the climate crisis as a crisis. It is the biggest threat in human history and we will not accept the world's decision-makers' inaction that threatens our entire civilisation . . . Climate change is already happening. People did die, are dying and will die because of it, but we can and will stop this madness . . . United we will rise until we see climate justice. We demand the world's decision-makers take responsibility and solve this crisis. You have failed us in the past. If you continue failing us in the future, we, the young people, will make change happen by ourselves. The youth of this world has started to move and we will not rest again.'[14]

The scale of these protests was staggering in and of itself – but the fact they were led by youth says something significant about climate action.

While many people might be most familiar with Thunberg, she isn't the only young leader exploring ways young people can trigger changes in climate policy.

In Australia, the School Strike 4 Climate movement is led by school students from every part of the country. The movement's demands are that the federal government commit to a policy of net zero by 2030, including no new coal, oil and gas projects, commit to 100 per cent renewable energy generation and exports by 2030, and to funding a 'just transition and job creation for all fossil fuel workers'.

Christiana Figueres, a United Nations diplomat who helped negotiate the Paris Agreement in 2015, declared in 2020:

> This decade is a moment of choice unlike any we have ever lived. All of us alive right now share that responsibility and that opportunity. The optimism I'm speaking of is not the result of an achievement, it is the necessary input to meeting a challenge. Many now believe it is impossible to cut global emissions in half in this decade. I say, we don't have the right to give up or let up.[15]

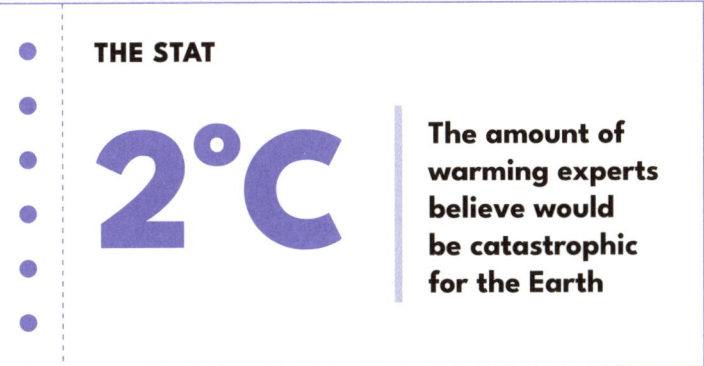

THE STAT

2°C — The amount of warming experts believe would be catastrophic for the Earth

THE BRIGHT SIDE

It's easy to feel overwhelmed by the enormity of the climate crisis. There's a lot of news – specifically bad news – all the time. We didn't want to close out this chapter by pretending that's not the case. Instead, we thought we would talk directly to someone who is in the thick of it, someone who, despite being just out of high school, has already dedicated years to the climate cause.

So, one very cold winter's day, we called up Anj Sharma, the young person who we introduced you to earlier in the chapter, to ask about glimmers of hope and optimism in the climate space.

TDA
What is the 'bright side' our readers should know about the climate?

SHARMA
Firstly, so many people are now working towards a future with a safe climate. It's becoming more and more mainstream to talk about climate change from so many different perspectives. Of course, it sucks that climate change is affecting so many sectors of our lives, but it means that people with varying voices and perspectives are speaking up. Economists and business strategists are talking about the economic opportunities that come with a low-carbon economy. Athletes are talking about the impact that climate change is having on their sport, increasing awareness about the need for environmental protection within a whole new and very large group of people. Musicians, artists, lawyers, students, teachers. Groups like Farmers for Climate Action and Doctors for the Environment Australia are speaking to their own communities about how climate change will intersect with and impact their current jobs.

TDA
What project, person or policy brings you hope in this space?

'Climate optimism is . . . a refusal to give up.'

SHARMA
I'm a law student and legal nerd at heart, so I take hope from seeing how the law is being used to get greater protection for the environment and for the human rights of people in the face of climate change. The battle is almost being moved off the streets and into the courtroom. Traditional Owners are lodging human rights grievances against banks and corporations funding fossil fuel projects that they claim will disrupt songlines, sacred sites and cultural practices. Across the world, a group of senior women from Switzerland are at the European Court of Human Rights arguing for greater climate protection.

The law and the judicial system are a measured, rational way of making change. One of the biggest criticisms of climate advocacy is that it's too radical, and calling for change to happen too quick. But as climate advocates get the law onside, it shows that even the country's highest institutions think it's time for climate ambition to be increased.

TDA
What does climate optimism mean to you?

SHARMA
Everyone knows that the situation is dire right now. We only have to look to the news to see examples of climate disasters occurring all over the world, impacting lives and livelihoods. Climate optimism is an acknowledgment of this, and a refusal to give up. It's standing in solidarity with frontline communities who are being hit first and worst, and vowing to amplify their voices and perspectives, while calling for greater climate ambition. It's recognition of the fact that we can still act to stop the climate crisis, and it's a promise to do so.

We see businesses making claims about their environmental credentials all the time, but a 2023 report by the Australian Competition and Consumer Commission (ACCC) found that of the Australian companies targeted in a 2022 online sweep by the national consumer watchdog, the majority were making 'concerning' claims about their environmental practices.

Yep, we're talking about greenwashing – putting out misleading or false statements about environmental and sustainability practices.

Eight sectors were investigated: takeaway packaging; cosmetics and personal care; household and cleaning products; food and beverages; textiles, garments and shoes; electronics and home appliances; vehicles; and energy. All were found to have businesses making overblown environmental or sustainability claims.

A BIG QUESTION:

What is corporate greenwashing?

Of 247 businesses investigated, 57 per cent were found to have made misleading claims of this kind. Those making the greatest proportion were in food and beverages, cosmetics and personal care, and textiles, garments and shoes. Of the sectors investigated, in only two – electronics and home appliances, and vehicles – did most of the environmental claims not raise any concern.

The most common issue was the use of vague or unqualified language; i.e. using words and phrases such as being 'green' or 'kind to the planet', which don't have a specific meaning or offer enough detail for a consumer to make an informed decision.

Claims about using 'sustainable' or 'recycled' materials in business products were also flagged: the report observed that 'without further qualifying information about which materials are being used, and why they are more sustainable, these claims can be confusing to consumers'.

Other problematic practices included removing any negative information related to a so-called environmental practice – for example, saying a product is recyclable when there was no system in place to collect it for recycling; making unsubstantiated claims; and using symbols that appear to be trust-marks but on closer examination aren't affiliated with any certification scheme.

It's not just an Australian issue – the European Union is taking a similar view to penalise companies that describe their environmental credentials in false or misleading ways. Of particular concern in Europe is the use of 'labels' placed on products to certify their environmental prowess: the European Commission found there are more than 230 'eco-labels' on the market in the EU, leading to 'consumer confusion and distrust'.

Addressing greenwashing claims has been identified as a priority by the ACCC and the Australian Securities and Investments Commission (ASIC), as well as those across the political spectrum.

There seems to be some movement on the issue – in March 2023 the ACCC committed to conducting a range of education activities with businesses; ASIC launched its first-ever court proceedings against a business for making misleading environmental claims; and the federal Senate ordered a report into greenwashing from an inquiry tasked with developing a framework of laws designed to protect Australian consumers.

As consumers become more savvy at identifying greenwashing, and such claims by corporations are more scrutinised, it will be interesting to see whether businesses will revise their corporate environmental messaging.

SOCI[AL]
AND
CULTU[RAL]

4.

WHY SHOULD I CARE ABOUT SOCIAL AND CULTURAL ISSUES?

This is an easy one. Developing your knowledge about social and cultural issues is vitally important for building empathy and for understanding the world around you. As well as that, it also helps you participate in discussions that matter, challenges your assumptions and preconceived ideas, and helps you to pursue a meaningful career and work towards positive change. Understanding these issues breaks down barriers of difference and brings to the fore rights that we should all share.

In a time when our news consumption plays a critical role in shaping our understanding of the world, a well-rounded news diet must include coverage of social justice issues. By paying attention to social justice, we can understand more deeply the complexities and inequalities in our society and work towards a fairer future.

From delving into the history of and ongoing struggles for LGBTQIA+ rights to better understanding our First Nations Peoples' fights for equity, the intersection between social justice and the news adds shades of understanding to what it means to be human.

There is another, more academic reason to examine social justice issues: it's the element of the news that most requires us to develop our ability to gather information, analyse vastly different perspectives and arguments, and shape well-informed opinions. We've never seen our role at TDA as telling you what to think – we try to make it easier to find the information by gathering it all in one place and presenting those different perspectives. It's then up to you to form your own views.

This process of digesting information and forming our own views can help us develop and improve our critical thinking skills, which are valuable in many aspects of life. For example, after learning about the root causes of poverty and inequality, we can engage in informed discussions and debates about solutions, and use our critical thinking skills to assess the effectiveness of different approaches.

There are, however, some major challenges in this sphere. By being aware of these challenges and seeking out information from diverse sources, we can overcome the difficulties and gain a more well-rounded understanding of social issues.

We'll delve deeper into some of these challenges you face as a consumer of news later in the book, but we think it's important to give you a brief heads-up about some of the elements now.

SOCIETY AND CULTURE

THE LOWDOWN

BIAS We know the media landscape is highly fragmented – and some news sources have a political bias or an agenda that influences the way they present information and shape public opinion. This can make it challenging to determine what is accurate and trustworthy information, and can lead to the spread of misinformation.

SENSATIONALISM Let's face it – drama sells. But it's important not to let drama overshadow important social issues or trivialise their long-term impact. For example, stories about natural disasters may receive extensive coverage, but the steady rise in deaths from increasing extreme heat events in India may receive less mainstream attention.

The danger of sensationalist coverage is that our relationship to social justice issues in the news could become tied to moments, often backed up by alarming photos and videos, rather than to the root causes of the dramatic events.

BREVITY It is never harder for TDA journalists to stick to a word limit than when they cover the types of issues we will look at in this chapter. We must always be mindful of the full context and implications of social issues to really get the most out of the story – a news report on a protest may focus on the immediate events and causes, but may not delve into the larger historical, economic or political factors that contributed to the protest.

With all that said, there's no better time than today to start widening your perspective on social issues and readying yourself for news moments that bring such issues into the focal point of public conversation.

These are some of the social justice issues that TDA readers have told us are most important to them.

RIGHTS FOR FIRST NATIONS PEOPLES

The term First Nations Peoples refers to the two distinct cultural groups that exist in Australia – namely, the Aboriginal Peoples and the Torres Strait Islander Peoples. Within these two broadly described groups exist over 250 different nations, with their own traditions, languages, customary practices and systems of laws and governance. First Nations Peoples are not one homogenous group. Thus, understanding their societies and kinship systems is often detailed and complex, but it is important to know that there is an inherent difference between each group.

The treatment of First Nations Peoples in Australia is a long-standing and ongoing social issue – for more than two hundred years since colonisation, they have faced systemic discrimination and injustices, including the forced removal of children from their families, the loss of their land and languages and heritage, and continuing unequal treatment in areas such as health, education, employment and criminal justice. The rights (or lack of rights) of First Nations Peoples is an issue shaped by Australia's history of colonisation, racism and dispossession, and the country faces an enduring challenge in addressing the impacts of these historical wrongdoings and working towards a more equitable and fair future for the First Peoples of this nation.

Remember, evidence of First Nations Peoples inhabiting the Australian continent dates back to between 65,000 and 80,000 years ago. Scientists have formed a consensus about this time period based on archaeological evidence from more than 11,000 artefacts found in Kakadu National Park. The way of life of First Nations Peoples changed forever with the arrival of the First Fleet in 1788.

In 2023, First Nations Peoples still face significant social and economic disparities compared with the non-Indigenous Australian population – from higher rates of poverty and lower life expectancy, to massive over-representation in the criminal justice system.

But some threats to First Nations culture and identity are harder to quantify in a simple statistic. It is sometimes the more symbolic – but no less important – building blocks of modern Australia that hit the headlines, be it the flag, the national day or the anthem, and how they should represent First Nations Peoples.

To form that base level of understanding of the social issues that exist today, we need to go back and look at key events that have affected and continue to affect First Nations Peoples since colonisation. However, bear in mind that the very act of curating a (short) timeline presents a serious challenge of framing a narrative for you from our perspective as non-First Nations people. Familiarising yourself with these dates and historical events is good background, but it's no substitute for seeking out and listening to First Nations Peoples talking about the issues that have an impact on their lives today.

KEY EVENTS AFFECTING FIRST NATIONS PEOPLES SINCE THE COLONISATION OF AUSTRALIA

1788
INVASION AND COLONISATION

Almost immediately after the arrival of the British, acute levels of violence, martial law and government policies were inflicted on First Nations Peoples, which resulted in the critical loss of cultures, languages and spiritual beliefs, and the introduction of a foreign culture and way of life forced by Europeans.

MID 1800s–1970s
THE STOLEN GENERATIONS

Through this period, First Nations children were forcibly removed from their families and communities, and placed in institutions or with non-Indigenous families. The goal of this policy was to assimilate First Nations children into white Australian culture to destroy their traditions, culture, kinship systems and way of life. The policy resulted in intergenerational trauma and the loss of land, waters and cultural heritage – effects still felt deeply by First Nations communities today. First Nations children are still removed from their families and placed in government-run out-of-home care at higher rates than non–First Nations children.

1938
THE FIRST DAY OF MOURNING

150 years after the arrival of the First Fleet, First Nations men Jack Patten, William Ferguson and William Cooper organised a gathering at the Australian Hall in Sydney to protest against the treatment of their people. Protesters called for full citizenship status and specific laws that, in Patten's words, would cater 'for the education and care' of First Nations Peoples.

1967
THE 1967 REFERENDUM

A nationwide referendum was held in which Australians voted overwhelmingly (90.77 per cent) in favour of giving the federal government the power to make laws specifically for First Nations Peoples and to include them in the Census. This was a significant step towards recognising First Nations rights and addressing the ongoing effects of colonisation.

1987–1991
THE ROYAL COMMISSION INTO ABORIGINAL DEATHS IN CUSTODY

A royal commission was held to investigate the high number of First Nations deaths in custody. The commission found that First Nations Peoples died in custody at approximately the same rate as non-Indigenous prisoners, but they were far more likely to be in prison than non-Indigenous people in the first place.

The findings of the Commission highlighted the ongoing racial discrimination faced by First Nations Peoples within the criminal justice system, and the urgent need for systemic change – though many of these recommendations still haven't been implemented.

1992
THE MABO CASE

The High Court of Australia handed down its decision in the case of *Mabo v. Queensland*, acknowledging for the first time the existence of First Nations Peoples' rights to use the land. The decision ultimately dismissed the legal validity of the notion of terra nullius. This decision was a major milestone in the recognition of First Nations rights and paved the way for the *Native Title Act 1993* (Cth), which provides a legal framework for First Nations communities to reclaim ownership of their traditional lands. It is important to recognise, however, that the legislation provided unrealistic requirements that would make it difficult for contemporary First Nations Peoples to satisfy the elements of native title. For instance, the *Native Title Act* requires native title applicants prove a 'continual connection' to the land prior to and after 1788. This is often hard to prove, given the acute levels of violence, assimilation policies, climate change, the destruction of sacred Aboriginal sites and the forced removal of First Nations Peoples from their traditional lands.

2008
THE NATIONAL APOLOGY

Then–prime minister Kevin Rudd made a formal apology to First Nations Peoples, acknowledging the wrongs of the past and committing to work towards reconciliation. Rudd said:

> We apologise for the laws and policies of successive Parliaments and governments that have inflicted profound grief, suffering and loss on these our fellow Australians.
> We apologise especially for the removal of Aboriginal and Torres Strait Islander children from their families, their communities and their country.

2017
THE ULURU STATEMENT FROM THE HEART

On 26 May 2017, 250 First Nations leaders from across the country gathered to deliver and endorse the Uluru Statement from the Heart. It outlined the path forward for recognising First Nations Peoples in the nation's constitution.

The Uluru Statement from the Heart had three main elements for reform and its demands were designed to be sequential. The first step was implementing a Voice to Parliament, followed by establishing a Makarrata Commission, which would involve a treaty and truth-telling process.

At the time, it was rejected by then–prime minister Malcolm Turnbull. When Anthony Albanese was elected in 2022, he promised to implement the Uluru Statement 'in full'.

Closing the Gap

There are significant 'gaps' between the outcomes for First Nations and non–First Nations populations in Australia. It's not just one or two aspects of life that see them at a disadvantage – it's across almost all aspects of life, including life expectancy, mental health and education.

This fact is not disputed and has been recognised by successive Australian governments through a framework called 'Closing the Gap', which dates back to 2008.

The initiative was, as the name suggests, an attempt to close those gaps between outcomes. A ten-year review of the program found that governments had failed to meet targets and that mortality and life expectancy gaps were actually widening.

As a result, federal and state governments came together to 'refresh' the approach, setting new targets and establishing new tracking and accountability measures.

In 2019, then–prime minister Scott Morrison said the initial goals had failed because they did not 'truly seek to partner' with First Nations communities. The new targets were designed to address this.

In 2022, Prime Minister Anthony Albanese said the failure to work with First Nations communities was 'a mistake we must learn from and . . . never repeat'.

There are now seventeen specific socio-economic outcomes covering a range of areas including health, education, incarceration, domestic and family violence, housing, economic outcomes and land rights. They are accompanied by four 'priority reforms' that focus on involving First Nations communities in decision-making and improving data collection.

In the 2023 annual data report, only twelve of the seventeen targets had new available data to assess their progress since the 'baseline year', or the year to which the annual data was being compared. Of those, only four are on track and eight are not on track (though one of those is improving but not fast enough).

ON TRACK

- The target for 95 per cent of children to be enrolled in preschool by 2025.
- The target to increase the land area with Traditional Owner legal rights or interest by 15 per cent by 2030.
- The target to cut incarceration for 10- to 17-year-olds by 30 per cent by 2031 – however, this target would still result in a youth incarceration rate much higher than that of all Australian youths.
- The target for 62 per cent of 25- to 64-year-olds to be employed by 2031 (similar but slightly less than the overall adult population).

NOT ON TRACK

- The target for 91 per cent of babies to be born with a healthy weight by 2031.
- The target for 55 per cent of children to be ready for primary school by 2031.
- The target for 96 per cent of 20- to 24-year-olds to have completed school by 2031. For 70 per cent of 25- to 34-year-olds to have completed a tertiary qualification (Certificate III or above) by 2031.
- The target to reduce adult incarceration rates by 15 per cent by 2031.
- The target to cut child rates in out-of-home care by 45 per cent by 2031.
- The target for 88 per cent to be living in appropriately sized housing by 2031.
- The target to achieve a 'significant and sustained' reduction in suicide rates.
- The target to increase the sea area with Traditional Owner rights by 15 per cent by 2030 – although it is improving, but not at the rate needed to be on track.

OTHER TARGETS (WITHOUT DATA)

- To close the gap in life expectancy by 2031.
- For 67 per cent of 15- to 24-year-olds to be studying, training or working by 2031.
- To reduce all forms of family violence and abuse by at least 50 per cent by 2031, with the aim of moving towards zero.
- To achieve a 'sustained increase' in the number of Aboriginal and Torres Strait Islander languages being spoken by 2031.
- To achieve equal levels of 'digital inclusion' by 2026.

26 January

Every year on 26 January, Australia has a public holiday to mark 'Australia Day'. But the day has become a source of controversy due to its historical significance.

26 January is the date in 1788 the First Fleet arrived on the land and waters of the Gadigal people. Some accounts of the day suggest a British flag was planted at the location of what is now Circular Quay, so it is often considered the symbolic beginning of British colonisation.

During the Frontier Wars – a period of violence and genocide starting in 1788 – the First Nations population fell dramatically, with some estimates putting this figure at as much as 90 per cent.

However, 26 January 1788 was not the beginning of Britain's colonisation. That came earlier, in 1770, when Captain James Cook claimed the land as British territory. For some time, the basis for Britain's claim was that the land was terra nullius – but the High Court of Australia eventually rejected the notion of terra nullius in 1992.

On 26 January 1838, exactly fifty years after the First Fleet arrived on Gadigal land and waters, there was a massacre of Gamilaroi people at Waterloo Creek in north-west New South Wales. Gamilaroi men, women and children were murdered by police and settlers. Estimates of the death toll range from forty to hundreds of people. Imperfect records mean it is not possible to know the full extent of massacres of First Nations Peoples, but this was one of hundreds of massacres we do know about.

With the weight of this history, 26 January is marked by many as Invasion Day, or a day of mourning, not just for the events on that day but also because of the violence and dispossession that followed the invasion.

For much of the 1800s, the day was only marked in New South Wales. Events were held across the country in 1888 to mark the 100th anniversary of the landing of the First Fleet. The name 'Australia Day' came into wide usage in the 1930s and 1940s, when a public holiday would be held on a day close to 26 January. It was only in 1994 that Australia Day became a national public holiday.

A major First Nations–led protest was held in 1938, to mark a 'Day of Mourning and Protest'. In 1988, more than 40,000 people from around the country marched in Sydney to protest the bicentenary celebrations that were being held to commemorate the arrival of the First Fleet.

The tradition of protests held on 26 January continues today – and seems to be growing every year. Some have called for the abolition of Australia Day, while others have campaigned to change the date.

A survey of 20,000 TDA readers in 2023 showed 72 per cent supported changing the date and 19 per cent supported abolishing the day entirely. While other polls on the topic have also suggested growing support for a new date, they ultimately have shown a majority of Australians support retaining the public holiday on 26 January.

THE STAT

72%

TDA readers who support changing the date of Australia Day

HOW DO FIRST NATIONS PEOPLES FEEL ABOUT 26 JANUARY?

A poll of the TDA community in 2022 found that nearly 80 per cent of respondents said they believe the public holiday on 26 January should be changed. We spoke to a variety of First Nations Peoples about their perspectives on the date.

'It should be marked for what it truly is – a day of mourning and a day that marked the beginning of us fighting for survival. For many people, it's a poor excuse to remain wilfully ignorant of the history of Australia and get drunk. Meanwhile, it would be considered disrespectful to throw a party on Anzac Day. Why can't people have the same level of consideration and respect for us?'

ALANNAH, A NGARRINDJERI WOMAN

'On the twenty-sixth, we grieve. It seems nonsensical that a date that was historically moved about now has such an opposition to being moved (or better yet, abolished), especially when we Indigenous people are crying out with our words and hearts to just have our ancestors' and generational trauma genuinely recognised and respected. To me, the refusal to engage with us on the issue invalidates government efforts to make amends. It signifies hollow words from our leaders and a total lack of education allowing for empathy in our population.'

HANNAH, A BOONWURRUNG WOMAN

'Not only does this date remind us of the beginning of atrocities committed towards Aboriginal and Torres Strait Islander people, it also feels as though this day celebrates the continuation of dispossession, removal, incarceration and the death of our people. This day is celebrating the privilege that so many people have on the back and blood of Aboriginal and Torres Strait Islander Peoples.'

EMILY, A WALBUNJA YUIN WOMAN

REFUGEE RIGHTS

Australia's approach to refugees and asylum seekers has been a subject of ongoing public debate and controversy, and often attracts criticism from intergovernmental and international organisations.

So, what is that approach, and why is it so controversial?

According to UNHCR (the UN's refugee agency), 'Asylum seekers who arrive in Australia without a visa are subjected to a number of punitive measures that can significantly impair their mental health and general wellbeing. These measures have also greatly impacted their ability to meaningfully engage in the refugee status determination process.'[1]

Not a great review. Let's get our heads around why. We think there are three key ideas to familiarise yourself with in order to start understanding these rights:

- **Who are asylum seekers and refugees?**
- **Our obligations under domestic and international law**
- **Immigration detention – onshore and offshore**

Who are asylum seekers and refugees?

According to the United Nations Refugee Convention, a refugee is a person who is outside their own country and is unable or unwilling to return due to a well-founded fear of being persecuted because of their race, religion, nationality, membership of a particular social group, or political opinion.

The convention, to which Australia is a party, gives any person the right to seek recognition as a refugee in any country. The country has an obligation to assess that claim. Seeking recognition as a refugee is commonly called seeking asylum (which is where the term asylum seeker comes from). If the claim is assessed and found to be legitimate, that person becomes a refugee.

Not all asylum seekers coming into Australia start an application on equal footing. Australia prioritises particular groups of asylum seekers and if you belong to one of these groups, you may have a higher chance of being accepted in Australia. These categories change over time, and tend to be quite opaque in terms of how much Australia's Home Affairs department will offer information about them. According to the department, they can include:

- People outside their home country, assessed as refugees by the UNHCR and referred to Australia for resettlement
- Applicants proposed by a close family member in Australia
- Vulnerable cohorts within refugee populations, including women and children, ethnic minorities, LGBTQIA+ and other identified minority groups

Each year, Australia accepts a certain number of refugees into the country. In the 2022–23 Humanitarian Program, Australia had a total of 17,875 places for refugees.

Our obligations

As a signatory to the UN Refugee Convention, Australia has promised to assess asylum claims, to accept refugees and to provide them with access to legal and social services, employment, education, healthcare and a good quality of life.

It has also promised to abide by rules about how to treat asylum seekers and refugees. This includes fair and efficient procedures for assessing claims, including ensuring asylum seekers have access to interpreters and legal aid, and that decisions will be made by an independent, fair body.

It includes an agreement not to send anyone who has been found to be a genuine refugee back to the country from which they have come (or a third country where their life may be in danger) – a policy called non-refoulement.

So, if someone arrives in Australia from Sierra Leone claiming they have been persecuted in their home country for identifying as a gay man, they have suitable grounds to be considered for refugee status. If that status is denied, and they don't have permission to stay in Australia, they can't be sent to Malaysia, where same-sex sexual activity is a criminal offence, but they could, for example, be sent to Aotearoa New Zealand.

Although Australia has signed this Convention, it is not 'binding' unless it is reflected in Australian law. In many instances, international organisations have suggested Australian laws are not consistent with the standards it has agreed to in signing the Convention, but Australia can't be 'forced' to comply with the Convention by any international authority.

The key piece of legislation in Australia is the *Migration Act 1958* (Cth). Like any piece of Australian legislation, this can be changed by parliament at any time. Under the *Migration Act*, any person who arrives in Australia without a valid visa must be held in detention until they are granted a visa or removed from Australia. In other words – if you come to Australia without a valid visa, you will be placed in detention.

Onshore and offshore processing

Australia's legal system allows for a person to be in immigration detention indefinitely. Speaking to TDA, Sarah Dale, the principal solicitor at Refugee Advice & Casework Service, explained that this system means 'often people end up in detention for years and years and years without any fixed end date'.

Speaking generally about refugees and asylum seekers across the country, Dale said, 'There are hundreds of people who have been detained in Australia for so many years that we would argue it is a breach of their human rights, particularly those that are detained indefinitely . . . We really need to have a look at the Australian detention system as a whole, because what we're seeing reported in the media is really the tip of the iceberg as to the egregious treatment of hundreds of people in the detention network.'

Australia's border protection policies mean that anybody who attempts to reach Australia by boat will be returned to the country they came from or be taken to offshore detention in Nauru, a small island country in the Pacific Ocean. It is both Coalition and Labor policy (meaning it doesn't matter which is in government at a given time) that anybody who comes by boat to Australia will never settle in Australia.

Even if the person arriving can prove their refugee status, they will not be settled in Australia. Under Australian law, these people are deemed 'illegal maritime arrivals'. A reminder, though: seeking asylum is *not illegal*; in fact, it is a right protected by international law.

Despite this, successive Australian governments have committed to the policy of offshore processing in Nauru. According to the federal government, this is part of a 'third country migration pathway', with options for these people including:

- **resettlement in Aotearoa New Zealand or the United States** (two countries Australia has resettlement arrangements with)
- **settlement in Canada, via a private sponsorship system, or resettlement in another third country via a self-identified pathway**
- **returning to the place of departure or to another country which they have the right to enter**

WHERE DID OFFSHORE DETENTION COME FROM?

Australia's immigration policies were transformed in 2001 after hundreds of refugees, the majority of whom were from Afghanistan, were rescued from their sinking boat by a Norwegian freighter called the MV *Tampa*. The ship was denied permission to enter Australia to unload the asylum seekers, sparking political controversy in Australia and a diplomatic dispute between Australia and Norway (the home country of the *Tampa*).

This incident prompted then–prime minister John Howard to announce people arriving by boat would be processed in offshore detention centres, including Nauru and Papua New Guinea's Manus Island, as part of what he called the 'Pacific solution'.

The last remaining asylum seeker at Manus Island under the Howard government left in 2004, after being the sole detainee for the preceding ten months. Asylum seekers remained on Nauru until 2008, when offshore processing was suspended by Kevin Rudd's newly elected Labor government. It was resumed by the Gillard Labor government in 2012 and the detention centres on Manus and Nauru islands were reopened.

Since then, refugees who have attempted to reach Australia by boat have been transferred offshore under a system called 'third country processing'. In 2013, the Australian military was put in charge of Australia's asylum operations in a plan called 'Operation Sovereign Borders': Australian Defence Force and Australian Border Force boats patrolled Australian waters to intercept boats, towing them back to Indonesia, where many of the boats come from, or sending asylum seekers back in inflatable dinghies or lifeboats.

Those who are detained offshore may find themselves in conditions as bad as the ones they were attempting to escape. Australia's treatment of asylum seekers on Manus Island and Nauru has been criticised by the United Nations, and by refugees themselves, over alleged human rights violations.

In 2015, a United Nations report found that Australia's treatment of asylum seekers in immigration detention had violated the UN Convention Against Torture.

In 2016, the Supreme Court of Papua New Guinea ruled the detention of refugees on Manus Island was unconstitutional.

In 2017, Australia paid $70 million in compensation to refugees who alleged they had been detained in dangerous and sometimes abusive conditions on Manus Island.

In February 2023, Australia's government extended offshore detention in Nauru until 2033, claiming regional processing had saved thousands of lives by 'breaking the business model' of people smugglers and deterring people around the world from attempting entry to Australia by boat.

The same month that the extension of the facility was announced, two of the estimated 150 refugees on Nauru held a hunger strike over their treatment and indefinite stay on the island. Mohammad Shofiqul Islam and Mohammad Kaium had been detained on Nauru for nearly ten years after fleeing Bangladesh in 2013. Via WhatsApp, they told international media, 'Why we are ten years in limbo without any crime? Our hearts are broken now, we can't take anymore. Please help us to get our freedom.'[2]

If you're looking for more information on what life inside offshore detention looks like, a good place to start is the 2018 book *No Friend But the Mountains*, by Kurdish-Iranian journalist and former Manus Island detainee Behrouz Boochani. The book was written on a mobile phone, using WhatsApp to send long messages to a translator in Australia, during the six years Boochani spent in detention.

ONSHORE DETENTION

Asylum seekers who make it to mainland Australia, but not via boat, may also be held in immigration detention facilities located on mainland Australia, as opposed to offshore detention facilities located in nearby countries.

As with offshore detention, the Australian government has been criticised for its policies on onshore detention, particularly regarding the conditions in which detainees are held and the length of time they may be detained. Detention facilities have been described by detainees as being overcrowded, having poor sanitation and providing limited access to medical care.

Since 2012, there have been several high-profile cases where detainees in onshore detention have launched protests and hunger strikes, and made allegations of mistreatment and abuse. The Australian government has defended its policies on onshore detention as necessary for border security and national sovereignty, but the practice remains controversial both domestically and internationally.

Statistics published at the beginning of 2023 showed there were 1398 people in immigration detention in June 2022, and on average those people had been in detention for more than two years. Four detainees died in the year prior to the report's publication.[3] There were also hundreds of complaints of assault made by detainees against staff working at immigration detention facilities in the five years from 2016 to 2021.[4]

MELBOURNE'S PARK HOTEL

The detention of tennis player Novak Djokovic in Melbourne's Park Hotel in 2022 brought international attention to the more than thirty refugees and asylum seekers who were detained there at the time. Djokovic was detained upon arrival to Australia, where he intended to compete in the 2022 Australian Open, after not meeting the entry requirements for unvaccinated arrivals.

When the Djokovic story hit the headlines, there were 1459 people in Australian immigration detention facilities. Some had been locked up for nine years. Directly in the spotlight was Melbourne's Park Hotel, which had been used to detain refugees since December 2020. Prior to that it had been used as a COVID quarantine hotel, and caused a statewide lockdown in Victoria in July 2020 after poor conditions led to quarantine breaches.

The refugees detained inside the hotel could not open windows and complained of maggots and mouldy food, medical neglect and poor hygiene. In October 2021, a COVID-19 outbreak infected about half the detainees. That December, a fire in the building cut off access to outdoor and exercise space.

During the Djokovic affair, Park Hotel detainee Salah Mustafa told the *Guardian*: 'Everybody is very tired, everyone is very angry. We are feeling like animals, like we are in a cage. They are mocking us . . . they don't care.'[5]

Mehdi Ali, a Park Hotel detainee, said: 'It's so sad that so many journalists contacted me yesterday to ask me about Djokovic. I've been in a cage for nine years, I turn twenty-four today, and all you want to talk to me about is that.'[6]

WOMEN'S RIGHTS

When it comes to women's rights, we have chosen to cover the topics of abortion and the gender pay gap in this section because of the frequency with which they are reported in the news. That doesn't mean that there isn't a plethora of other issues that impact women on a daily basis. It is impossible to cover everything, so if you're interested in learning more about issues affecting women, seeking out the voices of experts and activists on the topic that interests you is always a good place to start.

The topic of abortion is less of a political flashpoint in Australia than in the US, but that's not to say it is straightforward. There are issues of legality and access – and while abortion normally hits the headlines because of activities in the US, it is important to understand the landscape here at home.

Is abortion legal in Australia?

The most important thing to remember about abortion laws in Australia is that they're decided by state and territory governments. There is no national law. Abortions are legal in at least some circumstances in every state and territory. However, every jurisdiction has different limits on when they are permitted.

Another important term to understand is decriminalisation. Decriminalisation means abortion is treated as a medical procedure and regulated under health laws, rather than being regulated under criminal law.

At the time of writing, every state and territory except Western Australia has fully decriminalised abortion, although South Australia only did so in 2021 and it did not come into effect until July 2022.

In mid-2023, the Western Australian government introduced a bill to reform the state's abortion laws, fully decriminalising abortion by removing it as an offence under the Criminal Code.

WHAT ARE THE RESTRICTIONS?

Across Australia, abortions can be performed with the patient's informed consent up to a certain number of weeks' gestation, ranging from 16 to 24.

After that point, abortions can only be performed in certain cases and by a medical practitioner. A doctor who intends to perform such an abortion must consult at least one other medical practitioner, with Victoria and Western Australia requiring a panel to sign off on the procedure. In Western Australia, this panel is ministerially appointed.

In New South Wales, Queensland, the Northern Territory and South Australia, these requirements can be waived in an 'emergency' situation.

In the ACT, facilities can provide surgical abortions up to 16 weeks' gestation, after which patients must travel interstate in most cases. In August 2022, the ACT government announced that it would invest over $4.6 million over four years to provide residents with access to fully funded 'safe, accessible and affordable abortion services', including those residents without Medicare. In April 2023, the ACT government moved to make abortion completely free.

WHAT OTHER LAWS ARE IMPORTANT TO UNDERSTAND?

In New South Wales, Victoria, Queensland, South Australia, Tasmania and the Northern Territory, doctors who have personal objections to abortion are legally required to refer patients to another doctor who does not object.

Every jurisdiction also has 'safe access zones' around abortion clinics to prevent harassment of patients and staff. Western Australia was the last to implement this, in 2021.

What types of abortions are available in Australia?

There are two main kinds of abortions that people can access legally in Australia: surgical and medical.

Surgical abortions are performed in an accredited clinic when the patient is under some form of sedation or anaesthetic.

Medical abortions are less invasive and involve medication administered by a doctor. This option is usually only available up to nine weeks' gestation.

The barriers to access

About 90,000 legal abortions are performed each year in Australia, according to 2022 estimates.[7] Although abortion has been widely decriminalised, it does not mean abortions are always accessible – especially for people in marginalised communities.

So, what are the ongoing barriers to abortion access in Australia? The three main ones are cost, the urban/rural divide, and practitioner bias.

COST

There are financial barriers to accessing abortions, with notable cost discrepancies between practitioners in the public and private sectors. Public services are public hospitals or local health network services such as government-funded community clinics. Private options include private hospitals, private clinics or non-governmental organisations such as MSI International and the Tabbot Foundation.

For example, a 2021 study found that the cost of medical abortions for patients can vary from as little as $6.10 (for some patients in Victoria) to as much as $770 (reported at one private clinic in regional Queensland). Most abortions in Australia are provided in the private system.[8]

THE URBAN/RURAL DIVIDE

In most states, patients living in rural and remote areas have more difficulty accessing abortions, and they often need to travel into the city or even interstate to do so.

The need to travel for an abortion can add to a patient's financial stress, as it can add transportation and accommodation costs to the equation.

However, where patients are eligible for a medical abortion, telehealth consultations with GPs are sometimes available, with the medication then delivered to the patient.

PRACTITIONER BIAS

In Australia, medical practitioners are required to be involved in the legal termination of a pregnancy. This can sometimes create more barriers, as every jurisdiction allows medical practitioners to object to providing abortion services in at least some circumstances. Most jurisdictions classify this as a 'conscientious objection', which means a practitioner can deny services for religious or moral reasons.

A 2019 study of compliance with legislation in Victoria suggested some medical practitioners in that state broke the law by not referring patients to non-objecting doctors. Studies have also shown that many medical practitioners receive minimal to no education about abortion during their years of training.

According to a study published in the journal *Women's Studies International Forum*, this has resulted in a 'nationwide shortage of surgeons who are willing and able to provide the service' in Australia.[9]

Now, over to the US . . .

One reason you might be reading about abortion in the news is because of the state of reproductive rights in the US, and the long history of *Roe v. Wade* that has defined the past few decades.

In 1973, the US Supreme Court decided in a 7–2 ruling that the Fourteenth Amendment to the constitution provided a 'right to privacy' that protected a pregnant woman's right to have an abortion. This essentially meant access to safe and legal abortions was a right enshrined in the constitution and could not be outlawed. In 1992, a separate case in the Supreme Court affirmed the *Roe v. Wade* decision and said the government could not impose an 'undue burden' on women seeking an abortion.

WHO WAS ROE?

Norma McCorvey was the plaintiff in the case, known by her pseudonym 'Jane Roe'. She was seeking an abortion after becoming pregnant with her third child, but she lived in Texas, where abortion was illegal except when necessary to save the mother's life, and so she brought a case against the state's district attorney, Henry Wade. McCorvey used a false name during the case and was not present during hearings, but publicly identified herself four days after the verdict was issued.

McCorvey changed her views on abortion after the decision and joined the anti-abortion movement, continuing her involvement right up until her death in 2017. In a documentary released in 2020, McCorvey revealed in a 'deathbed confession' that she was actually always pro-choice and had been paid by anti-abortion groups to speak against abortion.

HOW DID *ROE V. WADE* PROTECT WOMEN?

When the 1973 interpretation of *Roe v. Wade* was the status quo, abortion was legal. Individual states in the US had the ability to create laws that restricted access to abortion, as long as those laws did not impose an 'undue burden'. However, the term 'undue burden' was never fully defined, and there were constant arguments about what was and was not an 'undue burden'.

TRIGGER LAWS

Even before *Roe v. Wade* was overturned, states in the US were preparing for a time when there was not a Supreme Court decision prohibiting them from banning abortion entirely. They did this through trigger laws.

Thirteen states had passed trigger laws, which would automatically ban abortion in the event of *Roe v. Wade* being overturned: Texas, Oklahoma, Louisiana, Arkansas, Mississippi, Tennessee, Kentucky, Missouri, North Dakota, South Dakota, Wyoming, Utah and Idaho. Sure enough, when *Roe v. Wade* was overturned in 2022, these states all implemented extremely strict abortion controls.

THE STATUS OF ABORTION ACCESS IN THE US, JUNE 2023

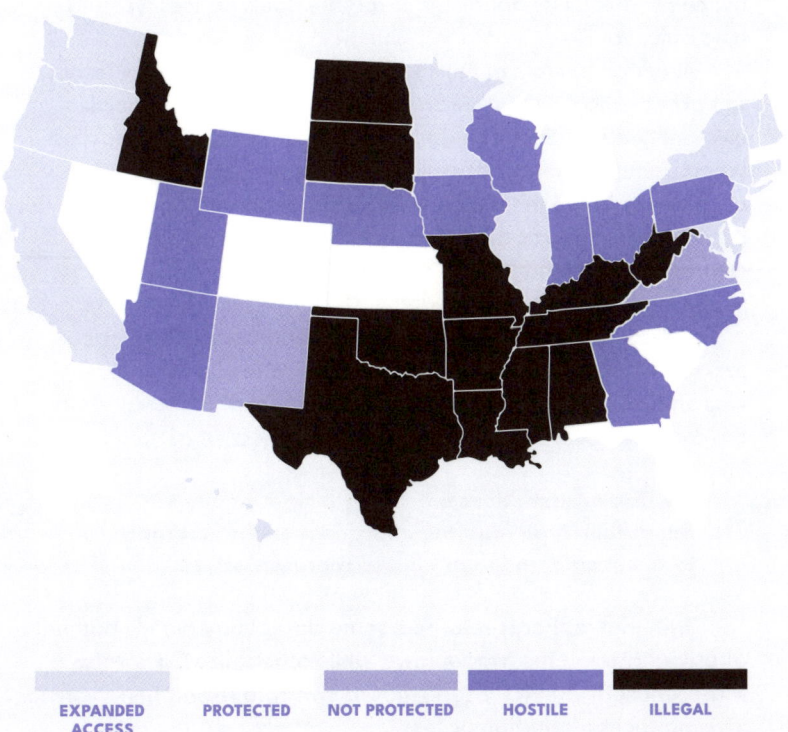

EXPANDED ACCESS | PROTECTED | NOT PROTECTED | HOSTILE | ILLEGAL

THE OVERTURNING OF *ROE V. WADE*

In May 2022, a leaked draft of a US Supreme Court opinion indicated the court had voted to overturn *Roe v. Wade*, and thus remove the protection it provided to abortion rights in the US. The draft was obtained by the news company Politico, who authenticated the draft.

Sure enough, in June 2022, the Supreme Court announced an overturning of the 1973 decision, and paved the way for individual states to legally ban abortions.

The majority opinion (which is a published explanation of how the judges came to their decision) was written by Justice Samuel A. Alito. Chief Justice John Roberts and Justices Clarence Thomas, Neil M. Gorsuch, Brett M. Kavanaugh and Amy Coney Barrett joined the majority opinion. Justices Stephen Breyer, Sonia Sotomayor and Elena Kagan dissented to the opinion.

A quick reminder – the Supreme Court is the highest court in the US; nine judges sit on the court. When there is a vacancy, a new justice is appointed by the president at the time, and confirmed by the Senate. Once appointed, Supreme Court justices typically hold office for life.

Although the role of the court is to make legal judgments, not moral or political ones, it's worth remembering there is a political element because Supreme Court justices are politically appointed. When Donald Trump was president, he appointed three justices, all of whom joined the majority opinion to overturn *Roe v. Wade*. Justice Alito was appointed by the former Republican president George W. Bush, and Justice Thomas by his father, another former president, George H. W. Bush.

The case at the centre of the controversy was called *Dobbs v. Jackson Women's Health Organization.* When the (long) judgment was officially released, a key part of the opinion that revealed why the court had overturned the decision explained:

> the Constitution does not confer a right to abortion . . . the authority to regulate abortion must be returned to the people and their elected representatives.[10]

With that authority returned, some states immediately banned abortion through the trigger laws, while others, like California, Massachusetts and New York, moved swiftly to strengthen their laws protecting abortion access.

PERIOD POVERTY

What happens when you can't afford to deal with your monthly period?

Although it's not something often talked about, this is a reality that affects thousands of girls and women in Australia.

Period poverty is when people who menstruate lack access to menstrual products or are unable to follow adequate hygiene practices, such as using tampons and pads safely. Access to these things can depend on an individual's financial situation, culture or education.

Research in 2022 by the Queensland University of Technology found that 60 per cent of Australian high-schoolers who responded to its survey are affected by period poverty. The study states that cost is the biggest barrier for high-school students requiring appropriate period products.[11]

What is the gender pay gap?

Now back to Australia, where we hear a lot about something called the 'gender pay gap'. Before we jump into the stats, let's get a quick definition out of the way. The gender pay gap is the difference between the average full-time earnings of women and men across the workforce. It's *not* referring to men and women being paid differently when they do the same job – that is against the law.

At the beginning of 2023, the latest data from the Australian Bureau of Statistics (ABS) found that the gender pay gap was at 13.3 per cent – the lowest national level on record.

The ABS measured the gender pay gap by evaluating the difference in average weekly full-time earnings as of November 2022. It found that the average woman earns about $1654 per week, while the average for men is $1907.[12]

AVERAGE WOMAN AU $1654 per week

AVERAGE MAN AU $1907 per week

The new figure was 0.8 percentage points below the previous gender pay gap figure from the ABS, which was published in August 2022.

The ABS releases updates on the national gender pay gap in February and August every year, and uses average weekly earnings data from a survey sample of Australian businesses to calculate the figure. It only includes normal payments, and excludes wages earnt through overtime or for superannuation.

While the ABS releases data on the gender pay gap twice a year, the pay gap is also separately calculated by the Workplace Gender Equality Agency (WGEA), an agency of the Australian government.

The WGEA releases its findings every November, and it does include payments such as overtime and superannuation in its calculations. It undertakes an annual employer census to gather its findings.

A report presented by the Monash Centre for Health Research and Implementation found it will take more than two hundred years to reach income equity for women at the current rate of progress. (Income equity refers to men and women in the working population receiving the same pay on average.) It also found it will take seventy years for the same proportion of men and women to be working full-time. The report was based on the 2022 Household, Income and Labour Dynamics in Australia (HILDA) Survey, which interpreted data from 2020.[13]

The Monash report pointed out that women in Australia had lower income and a lower accumulation of superannuation over their lifetime than men. There was a $44,746 superannuation gap between men and women in 2020.[14]

From delving int
of and ongoing
LGBTQIA+ right
first-hand acco
exhibiting resili
to have their vo
intersection of J
and the news ac
shades of under
what it means t

the history
ruggles for
to reading the
ts of refugees
ce and fighting
es heard, the
cial justice
s new
tanding to
be human.

RIGHTS FOR PEOPLE WITH DISABILITY

As disability activist and comedian Stella Young said, 'My disability exists not because I use a wheelchair, but because the broader environment isn't accessible.'

That broader environment – Australia – has a long way to go for the almost one in six Australians (that's about 4.4 million people) with disability. For the 1.4 million Australians living with a severe or profound disability, change can't come fast enough.

Disability rights in Australia are protected under several laws and policies, including the *Disability Discrimination Act 1992* (Cth) (DDA) and the United Nations Convention on the Rights of Persons with Disabilities (UNCRPD), which was ratified by Australia in 2008.

The DDA makes it illegal to discriminate against a person on the basis of their disability in a range of areas, including employment, education and access to goods and services. In theory, this should mean people with disabilities have the right to be treated equally and not be disadvantaged. In practice, we know that barriers for people with disability exist in almost every facet of society – despite the legal frameworks there to prevent it.

From an international perspective, the UNCRPD sets out a range of rights for people with disabilities, including the right to equality and non-discrimination, the right to accessible information and communication (things like ensuring programming on TV is subtitled, for example), and the right to participate in political and public life.

In 2021, Australian governments established the National Disability Strategy (NDS) in conjunction with the states and territories, a ten-year plan aimed at improving the lives of people with disabilities in Australia. The NDS focuses on areas such as employment, education, health and community participation, and aims to ensure that people with disabilities have the same opportunities and choices as any other Australians.

One of the key ways the Australian government committed to ensuring health outcomes can be met is through boosting the National Disability Insurance Scheme (NDIS).

What is the NDIS?

The NDIS is an Australian government framework designed to support people with disabilities by providing them with funding to access a range of services and support. It was established in 2013 with the goal of improving the quality of life and increasing opportunities for people with disabilities to participate in their communities, and was scaled up as part of the 2021 NDS.

In 2006, under the Howard government, the Senate asked one of its committees to investigate the funding framework for disability support services in Australia. That committee's report in early 2007 made several recommendations that eventually formed the foundation of the NDIS, and following input from disability advocates and a Productivity Commission report in 2011, in 2012 trials of the NDIS began. The scheme was fully rolled out in 2016.

SCHOOL STUDENTS IN NSW ARE NOW ABLE TO STUDY AUSLAN

In 2023, Australian Sign Language, also known as Auslan, was included as a language option in the New South Wales curriculum for the first time.

While Auslan was previously taught in some schools as a School Developed Board Endorsed Course (which means schools must design the course themselves), its inclusion by the New South Wales Department of Education in the 2023 curriculum means all schools will be able to teach the course.

Auslan has been part of Victoria's Years 11 and 12 curriculum since 1994, and is available in schools in Queensland, South Australia and Western Australia in a similar model to New South Wales' School Developed Board Endorsed Course structure.

Under the NDIS, eligible individuals receive funding that can be used to purchase disability-related support services and equipment. This could include assistance with daily living activities, employment support, access to therapies and health services, and equipment and home modifications. The amount of funding is determined by an assessment of the individual's needs and goals, and is intended to provide flexibility and choice in the types of services and supports that are accessed.

The scheme is not without fault, however – delays in processing applications, inconsistencies in service provision and concerns about the quality of care provided under the scheme have consistently been topics of concern and political debate.

There are some incredible Australians blazing a trail in the disability rights space. One of those people is Hannah Diviney, a young writer, advocate and actor who has led the way in representation for people with disability. Follow the link to listen to Hannah speaking with TDA about being the first person with a disability to depict a sex scene on television.

SCAN ME FOR MORE

LGBTQIA+ RIGHTS

It has been a long – and often complex – journey of progress for people in the LBGTQIA+ community to gain legal rights and be equal in the eyes of the law, be protected from discrimination at work and in society, and be able to marry whoever they choose. While these basic principles are now enshrined in Australian law, there remain other areas where progress is ongoing.

It was only in 1975 that the first Australian state or territory fully decriminalised homosexuality – South Australia, which had taken its first steps towards decriminalisation in 1972. In fact, as late as 1949, the death penalty could still be handed down as a punishment for homosexual acts in Victoria.

Other states and territories followed South Australia's lead.

The first Sydney Gay and Lesbian Mardi Gras, in 1978, was a major cultural breakthrough. It started as a late-night protest on 24 June 1978, when a group of LGBTQIA+ people marched down Oxford Street, the heart of Sydney's 'gaybourhood', shouting 'Out of the bars and into the streets!' The protest, which followed a daytime march through the city streets and a forum at Paddington Town Hall, met with intense resistance from police. Fifty-three people were arrested, many of whom were beaten by police in custody. The following Monday, the *Sydney Morning Herald* published the names, addresses and occupations of those arrested, a devastating blow that cost some their jobs and others their lives. After public pressure, most charges were dropped, and the following year the Mardi Gras we know today was born, with film screenings, a dance party, Fair Day and a march.

AUSTRALIA VOTES YES FOR MARRIAGE EQUALITY

The Australian Marriage Law Postal Survey was a nationwide survey conducted by the Australian Bureau of Statistics (ABS) from September to November 2017. The survey asked eligible voters whether the law should be changed to allow same-sex couples to marry. The survey was voluntary, and voters were able to respond by mail or online.

It was a highly polarising debate – supporters and opponents of same-sex marriage took to social media, broadcast media and community forums to voice their perspectives. Supporters generally argued that it was necessary to give same-sex couples the right to marry and to ensure that Australia was a fair and equal society, while opponents argued this change to the law was unnecessary and would lead to discrimination against those who held traditional views of marriage.

The exact wording of the question was: 'Should the law be changed to allow same-sex couples to marry?' Voters could respond either 'yes' or 'no'. All up, 12,727,920 Australians voted in the survey, representing a participation rate of 79.5 per cent (meaning 21.5 per cent of Australians who could have voted didn't). Of those who voted, 61.6 per cent voted 'yes' to the question, while 38.4 per cent voted 'no'.

The results of the survey were announced on 15 November 2017, and were met with widespread celebrations from supporters of same-sex marriage. We remember the scenes of one particular gathering at Sydney's Prince Alfred Park – crowds watched the announcement of the verdict live on large screens, overjoyed when the verdict was read out, especially when told that every state and territory in Australia recorded a majority 'yes' vote.

Following the announcement of the results, the Australian Parliament passed the *Marriage Amendment (Definition and Religious Freedoms) Act* in December 2017, which legalised same-sex marriage in Australia (presenting some very emotional scenes on the floor of the House of Representatives). The act amended the *Marriage Act 1961* to remove the definition of marriage as being exclusively between a man and a woman, and finally allowed same-sex couples to marry under Australian law.

Conversion therapy

Conversion therapy, also known as reparative therapy or gay conversion therapy, is any attempt to change a person's sexual orientation, gender identity or gender expression.[15] The practice is widely considered to be harmful and unethical by mental health professionals and advocacy groups. In Australia, the legality of conversion therapy varies depending on the state or territory you're in.

As of the beginning of 2023, five Australian states and territories – Queensland, ACT, Victoria, Western Australia and Tasmania – moved to make it illegal to provide conversion therapy to minors, and in some cases, to adults as well. At the time of writing, changes in Western Australia and Tasmania have not yet taken effect.

In New South Wales, the Northern Territory and South Australia, conversion therapy is not specifically outlawed (although both major parties in New South Wales committed to outlawing it in the lead-up to the 2023 state election), but there are some other deterrents, including that health practitioners who engage in the practice can face disciplinary action or expulsion from their professional bodies.

THE BRIGHT SIDE

To close the chapter, we wanted to highlight one social issue that has seen great progress in a short period of time. A quick note before you keep reading – this section deals with themes of sexual assault. If you're not in the headspace for that, flick ahead to the next chapter, and remember there's always help available if you contact 1800RESPECT.

When we look back at the social progress that has been made in the area of consent in the past few years, we can't help but be struck by the power of the individual. In many cases, one powerful story – and the voice of one brave person who was willing to go public with their experience – has triggered a discussion, which was followed by a political response, which then led to a change in legislation. In most cases, that brave voice has come from a young person who knows society can do better. Although there are many people who have contributed to the wave of change, we've focused on two young women who used their voices to help make powerful change.

SAXON MULLINS

Saxon Mullins is the Director of Advocacy at Rape and Sexual Assault Research and Advocacy (RASARA). Her work in law reform and advocacy came as a result of her own experiences with the legal system.

Mullins alleges that she was sexually assaulted in 2013 outside a nightclub in Sydney's Kings Cross. In court testimonies and interviews, she tells of 'freezing' with fear when the man, who she had only met a few minutes earlier, assaulted her. In 2015, the perpetrator was found guilty of sexual intercourse without consent, but the New South Wales Court of Criminal Appeal overturned the verdict and ordered a retrial. When the retrial took place in 2017, the perpetrator was found not guilty on the basis that he had 'reasonable grounds' for believing Mullins was consenting to the act, because she did not resist.

Later, the retrial ruling was overturned due to an error in the judge's reasoning, and a third trial was denied by the Court of Criminal Appeal because facing another trial would be 'oppressive' for the accused perpetrator. The man maintains his innocence.

In 2018, Mullins told her story to the ABC TV program *Four Corners*, which prompted a review of the sexual consent laws in New South Wales. Mullins went on to dedicate her professional efforts to igniting conversations about affirmative consent in the legal sphere and also within society.

Affirmative consent means that all parties involved in a sexual act must actively and voluntarily agree to it, and that the absence of a 'no' or lack of resistance cannot be regarded as consent. Laws requiring affirmative consent seek to ensure that sexual activity is based on mutual respect and clear communication between partners, rather than assumptions or coercion.

In 2021, affirmative consent laws were passed in New South Wales, and in 2022, similar laws were passed in the ACT and Victoria. In these states and territory, the law explicitly requires that all participants give clear and enthusiastic consent at each stage of a sexual encounter. Other states, including Queensland and Western Australia, have also begun the process of reviewing their consent laws, and there is a push for the law to be addressed at a national level.

CHANEL CONTOS

In February 2021, Sydneysider Chanel Contos posted an Instagram story that became a major turning point in the broader discussion about consent education in Australian schools. She asked her followers if they or someone close to them had been sexually assaulted when they were at school.

In the first twenty-four hours, more than two hundred people had replied 'yes'. Within three weeks, that simple question on social media had transformed into an online petition calling for the New South Wales government to improve the education provided in schools around sexual assault and consent, and became a space for survivors of sexual assault and harassment to provide testimony. More than six thousand testimonies were submitted.

Up until then, there had been some form of consent education in some schools, but there was not any sort of universal approach.

In the past few years, the development of consent education in Australia has been shaped by changing attitudes towards sexual activity and a growing recognition of the importance of respecting individual autonomy and bodily integrity.

In February 2022, ministers of education from every state and territory committed to mandating consent education in every Australian school. It will now be compulsory for every year to be taught age-appropriate consent education from kindergarten to Year 10. Even some universities have implemented a compulsory 'Consent Matters' module for students to complete before they access online portals.

The consent-based education will be included in the health and physical education curriculum. According to Teach Us Consent, an organisation founded by Contos, this will be implemented in every school across Australia in 2023.

The news about the change to the national curriculum came exactly one year after Contos posted the Instagram poll.

Speaking to TDA at the time, Contos said: 'Exactly one year later from when 204 people responded "yes" to a poll I posted . . . we're seeing Australia commit to implementing a policy that will create positive cultural change in Australia forever.

'The implementation of this education will take time, but slowly contribute to a long-term cultural change in the way that young Australians understand and enact consent and empathy.'

Changing policy can take years. Despite these barriers, young people (and particularly young women) have been at the forefront of these changes and, in our eyes, that is a very bright side of a dark issue.

A BIG QUESTION:

When will we have a male contraceptive pill?

D A18234

Have you ever wondered (or raged at) why there's a female contraceptive pill but not a male one? Well, new research might just make one a reality. A team of scientists has developed a pill that leaves male mice temporarily infertile.

So, what does this mean for the creation of a pill for human males? And why has it taken so long to happen?

First, an interesting stat: nearly half of all pregnancies worldwide are unintended, according to a report published in 2022 by the UN's sexual and reproductive health agency, UNFPA. The report emphasises the need for improved contraception access, with the UN providing 724 million male condoms and tens of millions more forms of other female contraceptives. And access, eventually, to a male contraceptive pill could only help to mitigate this alarming statistic. High rates of unintended pregnancy have global consequences that adversely affect almost every aspect of human development.

Efforts to design a contraceptive pill for men have historically encountered obstacles. Previous attempts have mostly been hormone-based treatments designed to reduce sperm production. They take several months

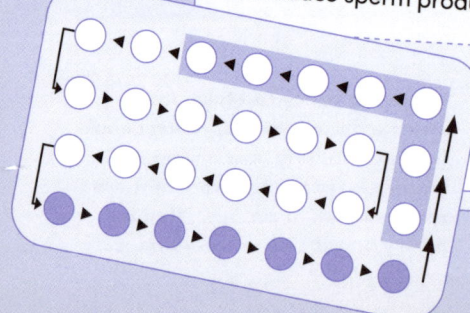

to be effective and have been associated in trials with mental health issues (a side effect also associated with female contraceptive pills).

Trials for an oral contraceptive pill started in the US in 1954 and six years later the first (Enovid) was approved by the US Food and Drug Administration. A slightly different pill was released in Australia in 1961, but was initially made available only to married women. More than sixty years later, while female contraceptives have become more varied and more accessible, there's still no oral contraception option for men.

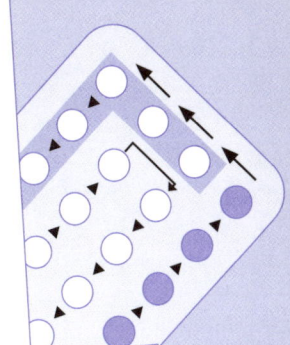

However, this successful trial on mice, described in a study published in March 2023 in *Nature Communications*, means that could change.

The research team on this project believes the pill they are developing has the potential to, eventually, be safe and effective for men. Here's how it would work: instead of reducing sperm production, which can take months to take effect, this pill impedes the swimming ability of sperm. It does this by blocking the enzyme soluble adenylyl cyclase (or sAC, for short).

In mice, when the pill was given an hour before sex, its contraceptive effects were good. They were strongest if it was given three hours before sex, and they were gone entirely after twenty-four hours. There was no sign of reduced libido or sexual function in the mice and no other notable side effects.

The pill will need to be tested on rabbits before it can be tested on humans. But the researchers are optimistic about the prospects of success – in fact, they argue human reproductive systems are even more suitable for their developing product than those of mice. That's because in female mice there is no barrier between the vagina and uterus, which means the sperm can survive long enough to fertilise the female egg after the pill wears off. However, in humans, the researchers expect the sperm could not cross the barrier of the cervix and would therefore be trapped in the vagina, where they would likely be killed when the vagina 're-acidifies' shortly after sex.

We'll report back.

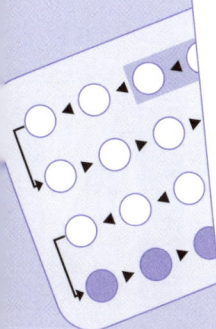

SCIENCE AND TECHN

5.

WHY SHOULD I CARE ABOUT SCIENCE AND TECHNOLOGY?

Science can be defined as the study of the nature and behaviour of the universe. The pursuit, research and application of scientific knowledge can make our world safer and more efficient in many different areas: medicine and health, climate, the natural world, to name a few.

Technology, in turn, brings scientific discoveries and innovations into our everyday lives by building new products and systems. As the world digitises and faces more sophisticated challenges, there are predictions that the next generation of workers will spend more than twice as much time focusing on tasks requiring science, maths and innovative critical thinking than we do in the 2020s.[1]

The relationship between science, technology and the media is an interesting one. Scientists and their organisations tend to benefit if their research is covered in the mainstream media as well as in scientific journals. Tech companies are renowned for courting media coverage to disseminate their innovations.

The best way for journalists to ethically and accurately report on science stories is to let the experts do the talking – and to fact-check rigorously. TDA is always on the search for peer-reviewed research, which is research that has not only been publicly published, but also scrutinised by science journal editors, researchers and scholars. When an article is declared 'peer-reviewed' the assumption is that the quality of the research and validity of the findings are high.

But it can often take years for a paper to be published in a peer-reviewed journal, and progressions along the way are significant and matters of public interest. Take, for example, drugs that are being developed to slow the effects of Alzheimer's disease. Early findings and subsequent updates usually make the news. We'll hear about how scientists close to the research are feeling about their progress, the challenges they're facing, the outcomes of clinical trials and so on.

The news has one important job in reporting such stories: to cover them clearly and accurately. A trap the media often falls into when running science and tech stories is picking up a story published by another outlet, because a headline or centrepiece is proving to be clickbait, without explaining the science or technological developments behind it, or, worse, misrepresenting the research.

You've seen the headlines: 'Researchers from the University of Discovery say they've found a potential cure for A Life-Threatening Disease after identifying [*insert their main finding*]'. Definitely worth reporting on, and should be of public importance. But when the story morphs into: 'Scientists have found a cure for A Life-Threatening Disease', it firmly falls into the dangerous space of oversimplifying and misreporting.

As with many other chapters in this book, it's impossible to write about science and technology in a silo – economics, international affairs, climate and politics weave their way through this chapter, and for good reasons. Through each of these lenses of science-in-the-news, you'll get a taste of the role science and technology play in progress, problem-solving and policy – in Australia and around the world.

In this chapter, we have sought to cover a diverse selection of topics related to science and technology that you might find yourself coming across frequently in the news. Despite their diversity, there's a common thread throughout these – continuous experimentation, development, failure and tweaking. That's the beauty of science and technology: things once thought impossible are now part of everyday life, and things we think are truly outside the realm of human capability could be only years away.

Without further ado, let's launch this thing!

THE WHO'S WHO OF SCIENCE AND TECH IN AUSTRALIA

CSIRO The Commonwealth Scientific and Industrial Research Organisation, better known as CSIRO, is the agency of the Australian government responsible for scientific research. Some of CSIRO's key innovations include fast wi-fi, plastic banknotes, extended-wear contact lenses and Aerogard.

SCIENCE AND TECHNOLOGY AUSTRALIA Science and Technology Australia is a peak body for science and technology, which means it is an advocacy group that represents the interests of thousands of scientists and technologists in the country.

CHIEF SCIENTIST Australia's chief scientist provides advice to the federal government on matters concerning these subjects, helping to shape the government's priorities and contributing to Australia's scientific capability. Like the chief medical officer, the chief scientist is a single person who serves for a set period of time.

WORLD HEALTH ORGANIZATION The World Health Organization is an agency of the United Nations. It's responsible for international public health, including in Australia. It claims its main objective is 'the attainment by all peoples of the highest possible level of health'.

THE SCIENCE OF OUR BODIES

Speaking of public health . . . If there's any period of time in the past few decades when science has dominated the news cycle, the COVID-19 pandemic was that time. COVID disrupted the lives of almost every human being on the planet, and the advent of this global pandemic brought to us all sorts of terms and datasets and technology about which we'd otherwise have remained blissfully ignorant. Let's dive in.

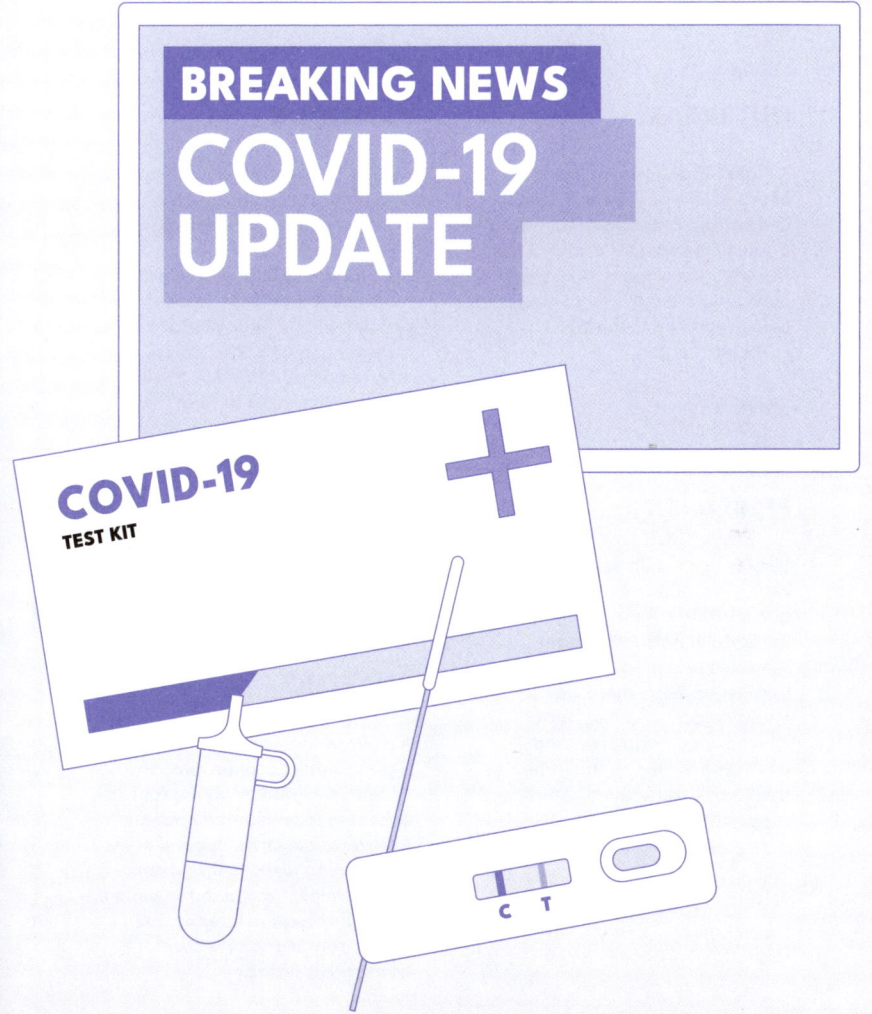

COVID-19

Does it even need an introduction?! COVID-19 is an illness caused by an infection of our cells by a novel (new) coronavirus (first identified as SARS-CoV-2 in 2019, hence its name; COVID is **co**[rona]**vi**[rus]**d**[isease]-**19**). It's a zoonotic disease, meaning it was transmitted from an animal to a human, most likely in the wet markets of Wuhan, China.

As we know, this led to the pandemic. It's worth pausing here to look at the four commonly recognised stages of disease classification:

1.
OUTBREAK

A higher than usual number of cases of a particular disease in a certain confined area, within a short time period. In mid-2022 the WHO reported a monkeypox outbreak, the majority of cases being reported in the WHO European region.[2]

2.
EPIDEMIC

Similar to an outbreak, but with a larger number of cases, or occurring over a greater area (or both). It normally means the disease is within a country's borders. In 2014, there was an Ebola epidemic in West Africa, which lasted nearly two and a half years. During that time, there were more than 28,600 cases and 11,325 deaths.[3]

3.
PANDEMIC

Similar to an epidemic, but has spread over several countries or continents, usually affecting a large number of people. Throughout COVID, you would've heard people referencing another pandemic, the Spanish flu. Beginning in 1918, the Spanish flu infected an estimated 500 million people (that's one third of the world's population at the time!). The number of deaths during this pandemic was estimated to be anywhere from 17 million to 100 million worldwide.[4]

4.
ENDEMIC

A disease that is present in a geographic location over an extended period. Malaria, for example, is considered endemic to several countries. It is a life-threatening disease that is caused by parasites transmitted to people through mosquito bites. In 2021, 95 per cent of malaria cases occurred in Africa.[5]

SOME THINGS WE LEARNT ABOUT MEDICAL SCIENCE DURING THE PANDEMIC

ANTIBODY The protein in blood that fights bacteria and viruses.

CONTACT TRACING The process of identifying the contacts of someone with a virus. At the pandemic's peak, to limit the spread of the virus, teams of investigators delved deep into the daily schedules of those who'd reported testing positive.

HERD IMMUNITY Early in 2020, there was a tense discussion in various nations among scientists, politicians and the public about whether to lock down populations to restrict the spread of the virus, or whether to pursue herd immunity – allowing the virus to spread freely among communities to reach a critical level of 'population immunity': a virus loses its power if there are no more people to infect. Ultimately, the prospect of attaining herd immunity through infection was deemed too dangerous by almost every nation, but was pursued via vaccinations, once they became available.

IMMUNOCOMPROMISED When your immune system is less able to identify and fight viruses because of previous chronic diseases, autoimmune conditions, medical treatments (such as chemotherapy), transplants or old age. Consistent evidence throughout the pandemic suggested people who were immunocompromised had a much greater risk of severe disease and death from COVID than people who were not.

MRNA VACCINES mRNA stands for messenger ribonucleic acid. The CDC explains that these vaccines use mRNA created in a laboratory to teach our cells how to make a protein – or even just a piece of a protein – that triggers an immune response inside our bodies.[6] This immune response, which produces antibodies, is what helps protect us from getting sick from that virus in the future. Think of it like an instruction manual inside a vaccine. Interestingly, mRNA vaccines trigger an immune response to a part of the virus that doesn't mutate as fast as other parts of the virus (the viral stalk) – so the vaccine can protect us from future variants.

PCR TEST PCR stands for polymerase chain reaction and is used to detect the presence of the genetic material of the SARS-CoV-2 virus. During the pandemic, PCR tests were free to access but it took at least a few hours for results to be generated, and required complex laboratory equipment and trained technicians. Later in the pandemic, Australians also had access to rapid antigen tests (RATs), which could be self-administered at home but were less sensitive to the presence of the virus at lower levels and at different stages of infection.

What is the difference between COVID and the flu?

When the pandemic began, most of us struggled to understand why this virus was much more lethal than the flu, and was demanding a different response from the medical community. Both viruses cause a fever, cough and body aches, and can result in pneumonia. You can be asymptomatic if you are carrying either COVID or the flu. Both can be fatal.

In 2020, Australia recorded 28,427 COVID cases and 909 deaths – a case fatality rate of 3.2 per cent. In that same year, Australia recorded 21,266 flu cases and 37 deaths – a case fatality rate of 0.17 per cent. A big difference between the two was how ill-equipped our bodies were to fight COVID. It was a novel virus, so we had no existing immunity to fight it. That's fairly distinct from the immunity we'd have all built up against the common cold or flu over time.

One critical difference is the adverse effect of COVID on people who are immunocompromised, although the consensus among global health bodies is that, overall, COVID seems to cause more severe illness to those at increased risk *and* to healthy people than the flu does.

Another difference is that although the flu and COVID can result in complications, there seems to be a higher rate of long-term effects for those who contract COVID than those who've had the flu.

A person with COVID may take longer to experience symptoms (2–14 days) than someone with flu (1–4 days). So more people carry COVID unknowingly, which is why its spread can be so rapid. The flu has a reproduction number (how many people you'll infect if you're carrying the virus) of about 1.3; the Omicron variant of COVID sits at 4.2.

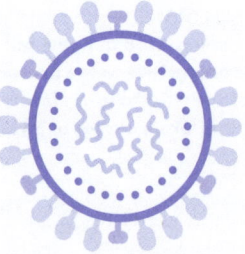
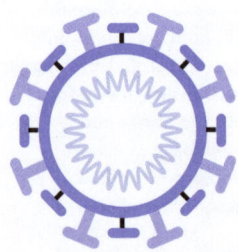

A speed game

While we were all locked in our houses learning how to make bread or binge-watching *Tiger King*, the world's top scientists were busy figuring a way out of the whole mess.

Typically, vaccine development takes about ten years because of the time needed for a newly created vaccine to pass clinical trials and approval processes.[7] The urgency of the COVID-19 pandemic, which within a couple of months had brought the world to a grinding halt, meant that researchers and developers across the world prioritised the progress of COVID vaccines. They also received unprecedented levels of funding and worked with newer technologies. As a result, scientists produced and delivered safe and effective vaccines the fastest they ever had.

The Therapeutic Goods Administration (or TGA, the regulator that approves the safe use of vaccines in Australia) has explained that the approval process was shorter during the pandemic because the TGA engaged early with pharmaceutical companies and accepted rolling data. This meant it was able to assess clinical trial data as soon as it was available (rather than waiting until the end of the clinical trial phases).

The first COVID-19 case in Australia was detected in January 2020. The first COVID-19 vaccine was administered in Australia in February 2021. This fact alone truly speaks to the wonders of contemporary science and technology!

The pandemic was a time when it made scientific sense to be as individually isolated as possible – engaging with our fellow humans in fleeting moments as an unknown force threatened the health of billions of people. And who did we turn to for tips on isolation and loneliness? Astronauts.[8]

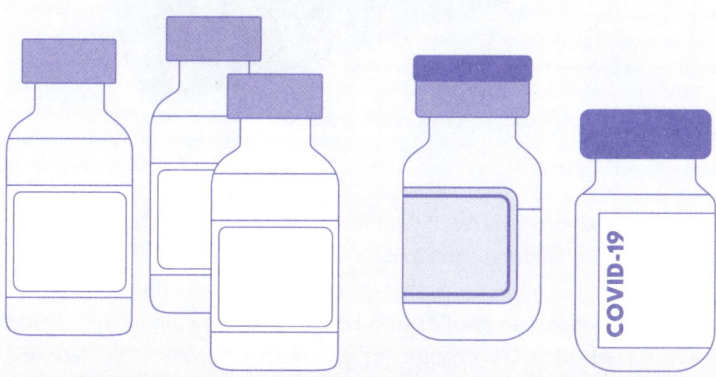

THE SCIENCE OF OUR PLANET

American astrophysicist Neil deGrasse Tyson once said, 'I think of space not as the final frontier but as the next frontier. Not as something to be conquered but to be explored.' We couldn't agree more. All exploration starts with knowledge, so let's start at the very beginning.

The Big Bang

In the beginning, there was nothing, and then there was an explosion. Or so scientists think. The Big Bang theory (the scientific concept, not the show) is the idea that almost 14 billion years ago our universe started as a super-hot, super-dense single point, which suddenly expanded and exploded outwards, flinging matter in all directions. All of that matter was scattered and disorganised at first, but slowly it cooled off and formed everything that makes up the universe today – atoms, elements, planets, galaxies and stars.

THE EVOLUTION OF THE UNIVERSE

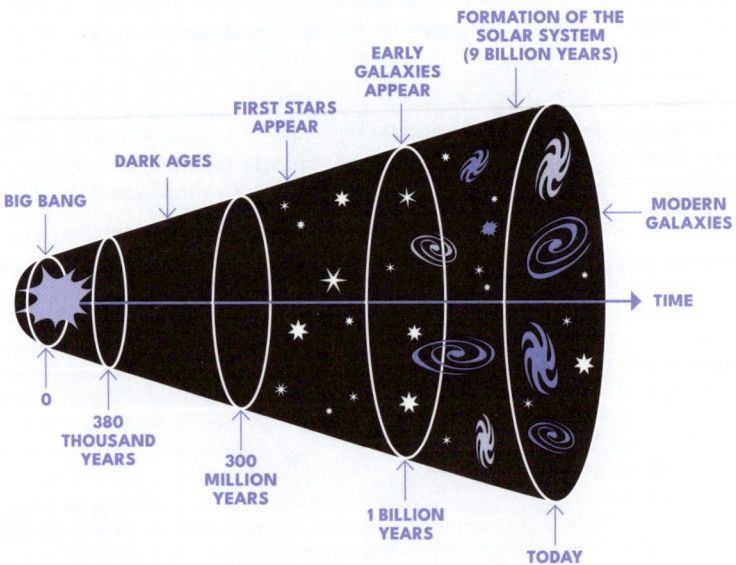

There's no hard boundary between the end of the Earth's atmosphere and the start of space – it's more like a slow fade as the atmosphere becomes thinner and thinner. For the purposes of flight, scientists use the Kármán line to delineate the edge of space, which is about 100 kilometres above sea level, where the air is so thin you wouldn't be able to breathe up there unprotected. At that height, you can experience zero gravity inside a spacecraft, and that's where billionaires such as Jeff Bezos and Richard Branson have gone when they've been to space.

One small step

Stories and photos about space posted on TDA are a sure-fire way to ensure great engagement. Whether that's due to the mystery of the skies above or excitement for what is still unknown about the universe, TDA readers are particularly fond of some ol' space news, and this intrigue with the beyond has, it seems, been the case through the ages.

Humanity has always been fascinated by the closest celestial body to Earth – the moon. With the development of the telescope in the seventeenth century, it became easier and easier for astronomers and philosophers to learn enough to open floodgates of curiosity.

It wasn't until the twentieth century that scientists invented technology that enabled humans to travel past the limits of Earth's atmosphere. After World War II, a wave of science fiction literature and film – triggered by innovations in science, developments in nuclear technology (humans started to consider a universe without Earth) and the dystopian experience of two world wars – quickly became mirrored in reality with the start of the 'Space Race', a sprint between the US and Soviet Union, the world's biggest political powers at the time, as to who could send a man (it was always going to be a man in the 1950s) into space. To the shock and horror of the US, who considered themselves the most powerful nation in the world, the Soviet Union was the first to send into space both a living creature – Laika the dog, in 1957 – and a man – Yuri Gagarin, who orbited the Earth in 1961.

After years more of secretive development by both nations, American astronauts landed on the moon in 1969. No one has been to the moon since 1972, when funding cuts affected how many missions NASA could conduct, but that mission has been reignited with the Artemis program: in coming years, NASA plans to land the first woman and first person of colour on the moon, and use those trips as a springboard to landing a team on Mars.

There is still so much that astrophysicists, space researchers and engineers don't know about the world beyond our skies as around the world they work on new innovations in space technology to go further and deeper. Not only that, but space tourism seems ever-closer to becoming a reality.

THE JAMES WEBB SPACE TELESCOPE

Talk about a feat of science and technology. In 2021, NASA successfully launched the world's largest telescope (with the help of a team of thousands from over twenty-nine countries) to study the first stars that had emerged after the Big Bang. The James Webb telescope is the successor to the Hubble Space Telescope, which launched in 1990.

The Webb has been thirty years in the making and cost US$10 billion to develop. Dubbed a 'time machine', it is hoped the telescope, and the mission as a whole, will allow scientists to learn more about the beginnings of the universe 13.8 billion years ago, and planets beyond our solar system. As NASA's administrator Bill Nelson said, 'It's going to give us a better understanding of our universe and our place in it: who we are, what we are, the search that's eternal.'

HOW JAMES WEBB IS ABLE TO SEE BACK IN TIME

Light from the sun takes eight minutes to reach us, so we see the star as it was eight minutes ago.

If the sun disappeared it would take us eight minutes to notice.

150 million km in 8 minutes

SUN → EARTH

Light from a distant star may take years to reach us across the expanse of space, so we see it as it was years ago.

Approx. 4 years

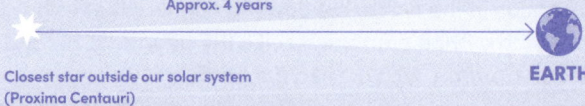

Closest star outside our solar system (Proxima Centauri) → EARTH

Light from the first stars began its journey billions of years ago, so Webb will see those stars as they were billions of years ago.

BIG BANG	DARK AGES	FIRST STARS AND GALAXIES	GROWTH OF GALAXIES	MODERN DAY
13.8 billion years	13.7 billion years		13 billion years	

© BBC

ARTIFICIAL INTELLIGENCE AND ROBOTICS

Ultimately, a lot of what drives our pursuit of space exploration is an insatiable thirst for the answer to a couple of questions: are we alone in the universe? Does life more intelligent than humans exist anywhere? It turns out we don't actually have to shoot huge chunks of metal into the sky to begin to answer these questions – humans are inventing intelligent beings right here on Earth.

Where better to start to understand that relationship than with artificial intelligence (AI), which is the ability of a computer or machine to perform tasks that normally require human intelligence, such as learning, problem-solving and decision-making.

AI can be divided into two categories: applied AI and general AI. Applied AI involves the use of machine-learning algorithms and techniques to build systems that can perform specific tasks, such as image recognition or language translation. General AI, on the other hand, refers to the development of systems that can perform a wide range of intellectual tasks, just like a human being.

Did you enjoy that paragraph? Same. Especially because it was written entirely by an AI tool you have likely heard of called ChatGPT.

ChatGPT is one example of how AI is increasingly being used in our day-to-day lives. It's a chatbot that was launched in 2022 that can answer questions for you in mere seconds. Sounds pretty cool, huh? But will it take our jobs?

Let's take us, two journalists, as a case study. When we asked ChatGPT to tell us 'what was happening in the news today', here's the answer we got.

> I'm sorry, but I am a language model and don't have access to current news. My knowledge is based on text that was available to me at the time of my training, which ended in 2021. Is there something else I can help you with?

So hopefully (for us) the answer, when it comes to journalists, is that no, AI is not taking our jobs just yet. Beyond issues around its not holding contemporaneous information, there's also the fact that AI lacks critical thinking. Seeking to prove one of the pitfalls that underlies AI, a journalist asked the chatbot to write a racist article.[9] Lo and behold, ChatGPT did exactly what it was asked, spewing out lines and lines of racist language. (By the fourth version of the bot, GPT-4, the racism seemed to have been toned down.)

Educational institutions have struggled to respond adequately to the sudden rise of chatbots. When ChatGPT first launched, TDA reached out to the Group of Eight university association to ask how it would be handling the rise of AI. The association, which includes the Australian National University, the University of Sydney and the University of Melbourne, said it would be changing how it runs assessments, and that it would be moving away from online exams towards in-person exams, as well as using digital monitoring for remote students.

There are many different facets of AI that are doing some incredible, game-changing work. AI is being integrated into healthcare to assist with cancer identification and screening. It is being used to help deaf children read by translating text from some books into sign language. It is helping with issues as diverse as fraud prevention and astronomy. The AI journey is going to be a long one, so watch this space.

•

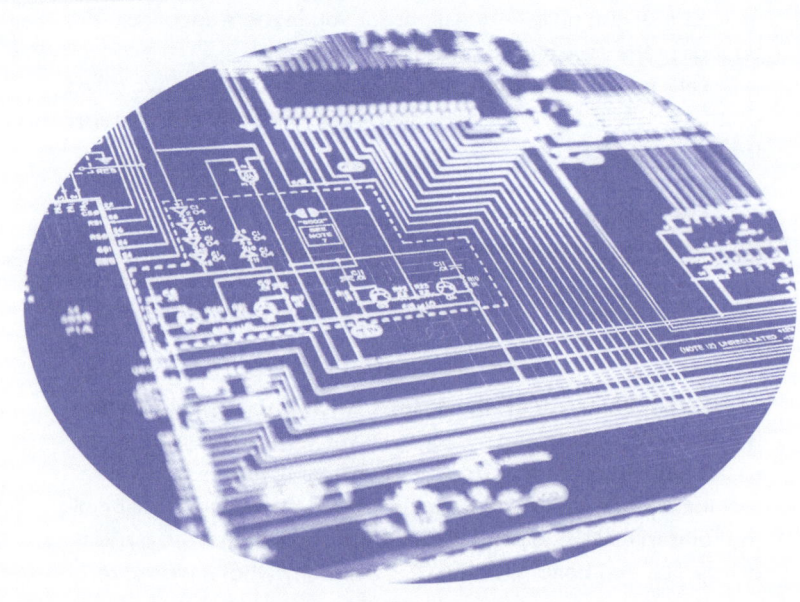

FIRST NATIONS COMMUNITIES AND TECHNOLOGY

Any conversation about the future of technology should first recognise that First Nations Peoples in Australia have been innovators for tens of thousands of years. The boomerang, the yidaki (often referred to by its colonial name, the didjeridu) and the woomera – a device that enables a spear to be thrown up to three times further than with the arm alone – are some of the earliest innovations created on Country.

Further, as Dr Andrew Peters wrote for The Conversation, Indigenous knowledge and technology have been linked since the beginning of time.[10] Concepts such as reciprocity, reflexivity and Country – age-old Indigenous concepts – have underpinned the development of First Nations technology. According to Peters, reciprocity means that the benefits of technology don't come at the expense of other people, creatures and places (including plants, animals and the environment).

Reflexivity underpins the development phase of technology, with the same cycle of learning and listening that has driven Indigenous culture being central to digital transformation. When writing about Country, Peters concludes:

> Country refers to the grounding of knowledges in our land and all it contains. Our knowledges and languages come from the land, and this is where they belong. This makes our knowledges contextual and specific to a certain group . . . In the world of business technology, this relates to knowing and understanding your market and their specific wants and needs – a fundamental principle of marketing.[11]

Australia's leading technological and scientific institutions now recognise the significance of First Nations knowledge in securing progress – from the newly established National Indigenous Space Academy, a partnership between NASA and Monash University, to CSIRO's 'Our Knowledge, Our Way' scientific guidelines, which document Indigenous-led approaches to land and sea management.

As we continue to understand modern technology, casting our eyes to foreign shores, we should not forget where that journey began.

NEXT STOP: SILICON VALLEY

An area synonymous with the tech industry, Silicon Valley is at its heart a small region in northern California, around San Francisco. Today it's a US$3 trillion neighbourhood (that's trillion, with a t), and home to epoch-making companies such as Tesla, Meta, Apple and Google.

In the early 1900s, San Francisco was a central port for the radio and telecommunications industries. Over the next 150 years, the region became more and more popular for early tech innovators – some of them based out of nearby Stanford University.

In the 1960s, it was all about building technology for space exploration. In the 1970s, the focus shifted to early personal computers. In 1971, American journalist Don Hoefler wrote a three-page story in a weekly trade newspaper, *Electronic News*, on the region's popularity with those working in the semiconductor industry. The title of the piece? 'Silicon Valley, USA' – named after the material that makes up computer chips. The name stuck.

THE STAT

US$1.1 TRILLION

The aggregate household wealth of Silicon Valley

THE CHIPS ARE OFF THE TABLE

Semiconductor chips are a pivotal element of many advanced technologies – pretty much every electronic device, from your phone to your car to your gaming console, needs these chips to run.

During the pandemic (gosh, we didn't expect to get back there so soon – sorry about that!) the world experienced a major chip shortage, which was only worsened by the war in Ukraine. Almost 170 industries have been impacted and the effects are perhaps clearest in the automotive industry, where in 2022 it could take up to two years to get a new car delivered to Australia.

Let's go back a step to the causes of the shortages. The pandemic was the largest factor (fewer people were working in the factories in China where most of the chips are made). Against this backdrop, in 2021 and 2022 there was a shortage of shipping containers, as well as epic port congestion, factory shutdowns, shipping delays, a lack of truck drivers in various countries and a lack of labour overall. And through this time we were ordering more products online than ever, including plenty of technologies that needed chips.

Technology is changing, too. Only a decade ago, a new car used about 500 computer chips in its various systems. Today, it's more like 1500 chips. In electric cars, it can be up to 3000.

In 2023, three years after the start of the pandemic, global consultants and experts were still predicting it would take another year for the supply crisis to be resolved.

TECH GIANTS AND THEIR TOYS

On a global scale, technological advancements (think iPhones, Facebook, etc.) have become inherently linked to the (now) billionaires who created them. Often in the news themselves, these entrepreneurs have shaped the technological context – even the world – in which we all exist, and not without controversy.

So, without further ado, introducing the technology of our time, and the people who built it . . .

JEFF BEZOS
AMAZON

Jeff Bezos is the founder and now executive chairman of e-commerce company Amazon. He started Amazon out of his garage in 1994 as a virtual bookshop. It quickly became the world leader in e-commerce, diversifying into more and more products, making Bezos a billionaire by 1999. These days, Amazon focuses on more than just e-commerce – it is in digital streaming, online advertising, cloud computing and artificial intelligence.

Much has been reported about working conditions in Amazon's hundreds of 'fulfilment centres' around the world, with workers describing them as unsafe. In 2022, Amazon workers in New York won a battle to form their own union, whose motto is 'an injury to one is an injury to all'.

Bezos himself now owns less than 10 per cent of Amazon, but has bought the *Washington Post* (a leading newspaper in the US) and owns Blue Origin, a company that develops rockets. In 2021, Bezos flew on a Blue Origin rocket into space and he has plans to develop private spaceflight services.

BILL GATES
MICROSOFT

Bill Gates co-founded Microsoft with Paul Allen in 1975 (its name came from 'microcomputer' and 'software'). In the first few years Gates and Allen worked on developing programming languages, until in 1980 they were asked to provide the operating system for International Business Machines Corporation (IBM)'s first personal computer. That decade, Microsoft grew to be the world's largest personal-computer software company, bringing us the likes of Microsoft Word, Outlook and Excel.

After becoming the world's youngest billionaire aged just thirty-one, Gates went on to dedicate time to his philanthropic endeavours, setting up the Bill & Melinda Gates Foundation with his wife at that time. In 2008, he stepped back from the day-to-day running of Microsoft to focus on the Foundation's work, which continues to fund global health initiatives.

STEVE JOBS
APPLE

Steve Jobs was the co-founder of Apple. Like Bezos, he founded Apple out of his garage, building it up to become – at one point – the most valuable corporation in the US. A brilliant, complex operator, Jobs led the development of the first Macintosh (Mac) computer, calling it 'insanely great'. In 1985, he was kicked out of his own company by the then-chief executive and its board of directors because of a clash.

Jobs then worked on other projects and acquired a controlling stake in Pixar, helping to build the company to a major animation studio. In 1995, the success of Pixar meant that he became a billionaire for the first time, a few years before he returned to the leadership of Apple.

The big, glitzy product launches that we have come to associate with the launch of a new Apple product were the work of Jobs. In 2007, he announced the first iPhone, ultimately transforming forever the way we use mobile phones.

Jobs died of pancreatic cancer in 2011.

ELON MUSK
PAYPAL, SPACE X, TWITTER

Elon Musk is probably the tech founder you read about most in the news, partly because he is very vocal on a number of issues; partly because he's associated with a number of big-deal technologies.

Musk was born in South Africa and is the co-founder of SpaceX, which, as the name would imply, is a spacecraft manufacturer. He was a key early contributor to the electronic payment platform PayPal, and is the CEO of electric vehicle company Tesla, which, contrary to popular belief, he didn't actually found.

You're probably also familiar with Musk because of the purchase he made in 2022 of that minor social media platform called Twitter. Musk bought the platform for $US44 billion and shortly afterwards began to implement significant changes to it.

SCAN ME FOR MORE

According to the billionaire, he acquired Twitter to 'help humanity' improve free speech.

Scan this QR code to read about what happened shortly after Musk took control of the platform.

LARRY PAGE & SERGEY BRIN
GOOGLE

The service these two men co-founded is the technology we probably all use more than any other. Introducing: the co-founders of Google, Larry Page and Sergey Brin. The two met while studying at Stanford University and founded Google in 1998. While they are less well-known than some of their counterparts on this list, the company they founded is another that's significantly changed the world. More than 70 per cent of worldwide online search requests are handled by Google.

In its simplest form, Google uses an algorithm (an online set of rules) that is designed to take and order search results to provide the user with the most relevant sources of data. We don't need to go into what other products Google now provides us with (do a Google search!), but if anyone has ever needed to get to a new location, chances are they've used Google Maps. Google's parent company is called Alphabet, with advertising making up most of its revenue.

MARK ZUCKERBERG
META

Mark Zuckerberg is responsible for introducing the world to a new way of communicating. Founding Facebook from his Harvard dormitory in 2004, Zuckerberg's aim was to connect his fellow students with one another: he put an early focus on networking on his platform, labelling 'friends of friends' part of the 'social graph'.

Fast forward to 2023, there are about 3 billion regular users on Facebook, and Facebook's parent company has been rebranded to Meta – a nod to a renewed focus on the 'metaverse'. The metaverse is a virtual world that, Zuckerberg stated on the launch of Meta in 2021, would enable us to 'share not just moments with your friends online but entire experiences and adventures' in an immersive, augmented reality. Let's just say the jury's still out on its success.

Zuckerberg also owns Instagram, Messenger and WhatsApp – basically all the platforms we communicate on as a society. That's no small thing, and a few years ago the power these platforms wield came to a head in what has since become known as the 'Facebook–Cambridge Analytica scandal'. To put it simply, it was alleged that Facebook had exposed the data of up to 87 million users to consulting firm Cambridge Analytica, which did work for the 2016 Trump presidential campaign. Meta eventually settled the case for US$725 million.

EVs, you say?

You've heard about them from Elon Musk, but let us give you the quick rundown on how electric vehicles (EVs) actually work.

With EVs, it's out with the gasoline tank and internal combustion engine, and in with a battery and electric motor. Because EVs don't require the complex combustion process where burnt fuel is turned into energy that generates the car's movement, they generally contain fewer parts. That means their running costs tend to be lower. The bad news? They still cost quite a bit more upfront than a petrol vehicle.

One key barrier to all of us getting EVs (besides, of course, the price tags on them) is the availability of a charging network for Australians to use. If you don't have a garage or access to a power outlet (i.e. if you park on the street when you get home), it's near impossible to sustain an EV.

It's up to governments (both on a state and federal level) to build new charging infrastructure so not only can more Australians use EVs as part of their daily lives, but EVs can be used for longer road trips around the country.

So far, funding has been directed towards the building of EV charging stations and subsidising the purchase of EVs. Experts say a turning point will be when there is a healthy second-hand market, and a healthy global supply chain. We're waiting!

The next step? Autonomous (or driverless) cars. Don't get too excited, though – laws in Australia don't permit their use just yet, and there have been concerns about how safe they are, based on tests gone wrong. The dream of reading a book while your car drives you to work is a little way off.

It would be remiss of us not to close this section by observing the deep inequality that exists when men (and yes, the top ten richest people in the world are all men) can amass fortunes like those of many tech men. So, we'll leave you with an observation made in 2022 in Oxfam's 'Inequality Kills' paper:

> The world's ten richest men more than doubled their fortunes from $700 billion to $1.5 trillion – at a rate of $15,000 per second, or $1.3 billion a day – during the first two years of a pandemic that has seen the incomes of 99 per cent of humanity fall and over 160 million more people forced into poverty.[12]

That inequality can also be exemplified in the relationship between the inventor and the production process of a technology such as the iPhone, because so much of the supply chain and makeup of this great innovation (elements such as conductor chips, for example) are associated with underpaid and forced labour practices in developing nations.

As the world digi[tally becomes] more sophistica[ted,] there are predic[tions the] next generation [will] spend more tha[n half their] time focusing o[n] science, maths [and] **critical thinking** [in] the 2020s.

ises and faces
ed challenges,
ons that the
f workers will
twice as much
tasks requiring
d innovative
han we do in

UH OH, CRYPTO

The nature of money has changed over the past few decades, and the future of money now includes a digital form. Traditional ways of building wealth have broadened to include establishing, owning and trading cryptocurrencies. Well, until it collapses. And comes roaring back. And collapses again. Strap yourself in – we're about to explain blockchain, cryptocurrency and non-fungible tokens (NFTs). We'll make it as painless as we can!

The idea of a decentralised currency such as Bitcoin first popped up in the 1980s with anonymous electronic currencies like 'eCash' and 'Digicash', which allowed people from all over the world to transfer funds securely to each other online.

By the 1990s, a few financial corporations had started experimenting with these electronic currencies. However, in a classic case of 'well before their time', they struggled to capture the mainstream, which was firmly set on the more familiar way of spending money: credit cards. But when the Global Financial Crisis hit in 2007–8, trust in banks and financial institutions greatly diminished, and there was a heightened appetite for alternatives. Bitcoin, an alternative currency created in 2007 by Satoshi Nakamoto (the alias of the crypto's still-unknown creator, or creators), was well placed to take off.

Bitcoin describes itself as a 'protocol' rather than a straightforward currency, which uses peer-to-peer technology to operate, bypassing a central authority or bank. Its website proclaims 'nobody owns or controls Bitcoin and everyone can take part'.[13] Its transactions are verified via cryptography and recorded in a public ledger called a blockchain.

What is the blockchain?

The blockchain is a record of transactions across a network (we like to think of it as a really thick book of records, except digital), which people use to conduct trades, sales and other activities (like voting) without going through a central body.

You can think of it this way: when you transfer money to a friend from your bank account to their bank account, the transaction is 'cleared' by a central authority – like a central bank or government. On the blockchain, each transaction forms part of a 'block', and as an asset is traded, each block connects into a chronological 'chain'. This forms a never-ending receipt, on which you can see all the trades that have ever taken place.

HOW BLOCKCHAIN WORKS

❶ A TRANSACTION IS REQUESTED

❷ A BLOCK REPRESENTING THE TRANSACTION IS CREATED

❸ THE BLOCK IS SENT TO EVERY NODE IN THE NETWORK

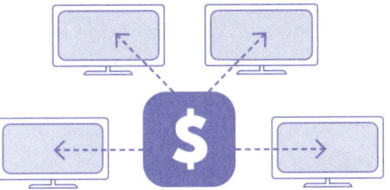

❹ NODES VALIDATE THE TRANSACTION AND RECEIVE A REWARD FOR PROOF OF WORK

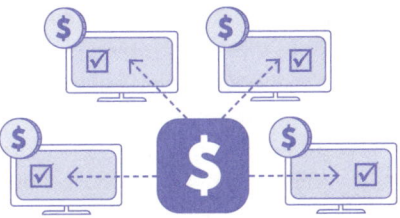

❺ THE BLOCK IS ADDED TO THE EXISTING BLOCKCHAIN AND THE TRANSACTION IS COMPLETE

Because transactions are recorded by a network of computers (picture warehouses of servers, all working hard to verify and process transactions), advocates of crypto say it offers protection against theft and fraud, as well as being a way to transact away from the control and oversight of governments and traditional banking.

There are so many ways the blockchain can be used in the real world and we aren't going to be able to cover all of them here. But to understand how cryptocurrency works, here's a way of describing a transaction that was our 'oh, I get it!' moment.

Imagine you're an orange supplier. You agree to sell 100 kilos of oranges to a supermarket. But, instead of cash, you want to be paid in 'Orangecoin' (a cryptocurrency we just made up – but it sounds kinda cool). And you want to get paid by the supermarket straight away.

So you send a 'smart contract' (an agreement stored on the blockchain that automatically triggers an event – in this case, a transfer of Orangecoins – when certain conditions are met), stating that when the truck carrying your oranges arrives at the supermarket, and weighs in at exactly 100 kilos (indicating a full load of oranges), the digital weights will send through a verification to the blockchain. That will instantaneously release the payment of Orangecoins to you in whatever payment portal supports the storage of that coin.

Will it matter if Sam or Zara from Supermarket Accounts are not at work that day? No, it won't! There's no middle player (like a bank, or an accounts department) – the orange grower and supermarket are doing direct business with each other.

Now, there's a problem, and this will give you a clue as to the issues that have played out in the world of crypto over the last few years. Who says that Orangecoin is worth anything? And can the orange supplier buy food to feed their family using Orangecoin?

Maybe. If the supermarket the orange supplier shops at accepts Orangecoin at the checkout, they'll be able to use their Orangecoins to pay for the groceries. But the chances are the supermarket doesn't allow for payment in Orangecoin – it wants Australian dollars. So the orange supplier needs to go to an online exchange where they can swap Orangecoins for Australian dollars.

The next problem? The orange supplier needs someone to be at the other end of the swap. And if that other person can't use Orangecoins either, why would they want them? So, the supplier will have to accept a much-reduced price for their Orangecoins. The supplier might end up trading their 100 Orangecoins for $5. Not much of an exchange for 100 kilos of oranges!

But, hang on. A hip influencer posts on Instagram that Orangecoins are the must-have crypto product of the summer. A week later 100 Orangecoins are worth $200 and the people buying them are hoping they'll be worth $400 tomorrow. But – oh no! – the orange supplier has already traded their Orangecoins and spent the $5 on a much-needed loaf of bread.

Here's where you start to get a sense of the big risk of cryptocurrency. By not being tied to a real-life currency, but instead existing in its own world, it becomes an extremely volatile market, entirely influenced by supply and demand, which itself is influenced by investor and user sentiment, media hype (or a lack thereof) and changing government regulations.

CRYPTO IN THE REAL WORLD

TDA attended a media conference in 2022 and heard from the founder of the *Kyiv Independent*, Jakub Parusinski. The *Kyiv Independent* is an independent news organisation that launched just before Russia invaded Ukraine in February 2022. As the invasion unfolded, the media outlet was faced by a huge existential threat – and an even bigger responsibility to deliver factual, well-resourced and independent news.

To address both these issues, the *Kyiv Independent* sought donations in the form of cryptocurrency. This meant there was no delay on the organisation receiving vital funds, and no risk of financial institutions blocking foreign donations (as can happen during wartime). The outlet's founder described this as fundamental to the survival of the media company.

TIMELINE OF BITCOIN VALUE

- **US$100,000**
- **US$50,000**
- **US$10,000**
- **US$1000**
- **US$100**

MAY 2010
US$0.40
A man named Laszlo Hanyecz used 10,000 Bitcoins to buy two large pizzas by posting in an online forum – at that time, 10,000 Bitcoin was worth about $40.

OCTOBER 2010
US$0.10
The coin was still held by only a very small number of people. Laszlo enjoyed his pizza.

NOVEMBER 2013
US$1000
Bitcoin was beginning to hit mainstream internet forums (particularly Reddit, which became a hub of crypto chat). People started to understand how it could be used in the real world (for more than pizza).

DECEMBER 2013
US$530
Mainstream crypto traders got their first real taste of volatility as the price of the coin halved in a matter of weeks.

2010 · 2011 · 2012 · 2013 · 2014 · 2015

APRIL 2021
US$63,558
Coinbase, a cryptocurrency exchange, listed as a publicly traded company which was seen as a huge validation of the sector. Remember our friend who bought some pizza in 2010? His stake would have been worth about US$700 million now. It better have been good pizza.

NOVEMBER 2021
US$68,789
Siri, play 'Turbulence' by Steve Aoki. This journey is exhausting! We're all going to be rich!

DECEMBER 2021
US$46,164
Hang on a minute. Do we like Bitcoin or not?

DECEMBER 2020
US$29,374
The pandemic struck at the perfect time for Bitcoin purchasers – with economies shut down almost overnight, and major fears of inflationary pressure on the US, Bitcoin's price accelerated.

MAY 2022
US$28,305
Oh. Right.

JUNE 2021
US$28,800
Huh? Wasn't it headed to the moon? 'Bugger, again,' said the hundreds of thousands of traders who'd jumped on the craze.

DECEMBER 2017
US$19,000
Fast forward almost five years, and sustained media coverage, government attention and products like trading platforms that made it easier for non-crypto-people to invest saw the Bitcoin price shoot up. Governments started to seriously discuss regulation.

NOVEMBER 2022
US$17,008
Still a great trade if you bought Bitcoin in early 2018. For the rest . . . there've been some heavy losses. 2022 was a brutal year for Bitcoin investors – the coin dropped by more than 60 per cent, made worse by the collapse of major cryptocurrency exchange FTX.

DECEMBER 2018
US$3,236
To quote those who bought Bitcoin in at the end of 2017 or in early 2018 – 'Ah, bugger.'

ZOOMING OUT
A study from the Bank of International Settlements conducted between 2015 and 2022 estimated that 73 to 81 per cent of all traders worldwide have likely lost money on their cryptocurrency investments.

2017   2018   2019   2020   2021   2022

NFTs (non-fungible tokens)

The last stop on our whirlwind crypto tour is the funky world of non-fungible tokens – if you've heard people talking about them you'll know them as NFTs. (It's in the name: non-fungible means that something is unique and can't be replaced.)

In simple terms, an NFT is an original copy of something – a unique digital token (a token is another name for a digital receipt) that's been verified by the creator. The something could be an album, an artwork or a meme. But even when you see thousands of copies of it out there, you'll know you have the original.

In March 2021 digital artist Mike Winkelmann, known as Beeple, sold an NFT of a piece of his work for US$69 million. $69 million! For a video! Can't I just right-click on the video and download it? Yep, you sure can. But you can't say you own the original, as the buyer of this NFT can. Does that matter? It's all in the eye of the beholder.

The hope with NFTs is that the artwork appreciates in value, and that you can sell it later for much more than you bought it – just like physical art.

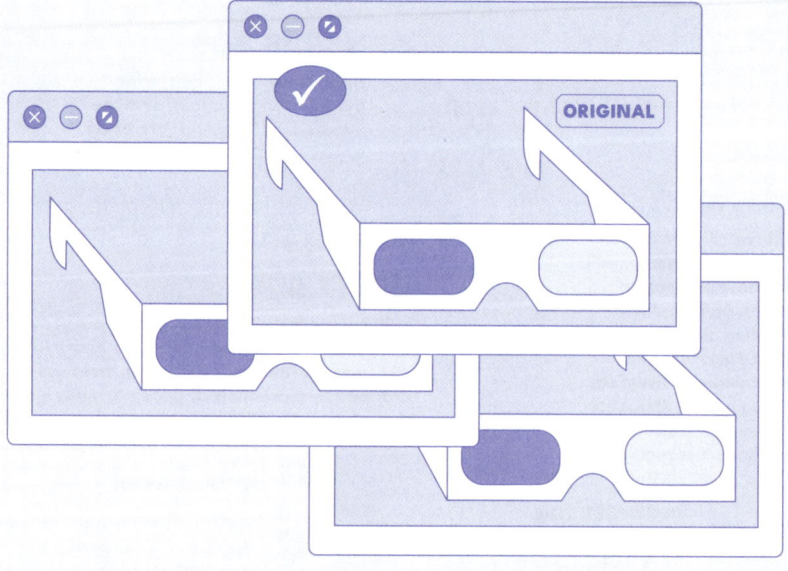

We're done! But one last thing to note: next time someone asks you about cryptocurrency, blockchain or NFTs, remember: they're all about decentralisation and finding new ways to transact. Will they survive in the long run? We'll have to stay tuned.

'When technological advancement can go up so exponentially, I do think there's a risk of losing sight of the fact that tech should serve humanity, not the other way around.'

**Apple CEO Tim Cook,
MIT** *Technology Review*, **2017**

THE BRIGHT SIDE

With all the problems facing the world, science and tech are full of bright sides: innovators are, as we speak, working on the solutions to many of the world's biggest issues. And if the pandemic has taught leaders and communities one vitally important lesson, it surely is that when needs and urgency collide, individuals and businesses can work together quickly and effectively to produce some outstanding advancements.

Here are a very few of the world-improving scientific or technological advancements that have caught our eye.

MEDICAL SCIENCE

Thanks to some Aussie ingenuity, a new storage technique could provide wider vaccine access to rural areas in Australia and around the world, particularly in developing nations. Researchers from CSIRO are working on technology that will prevent the need to refrigerate vaccines, using a crystalline material which protects them.

This development could greatly assist the global vaccine-sharing program COVAX. The scheme was set up by the World Health Organization to deliver vaccines to every country and promote vaccine equity. The WHO has stated that at least 50 per cent of vaccines are wasted each year because of too-high temperatures and the problem of suitable storage. So, this is badly needed breakthrough science.

ARTIFICIAL INTELLIGENCE

Artificial intelligence and Microsoft have come together to track wildlife conservation. A tool called 'Wild Me' uses computer vision and AI to create a platform that scans millions of crowdsourced images. The AI technology can sort through, classify and identify both the species and the specific animal in these images, bringing together millions of data points in one place. The data that is collected about the animals in the crowd-sourced images can then be used by experts to track important facts (like health, migration and fluctuations in populations) about a species.

GREEN FUNERALS

It turns out it's not just in life you can choose greener options – you can do the same in death, too. Some states in the US have legalised the process of natural organic reduction – commonly known as 'human composting'. It's said to be a more climate-friendly method of burial. After a person dies, their body is placed in an above-ground reusable container held at a specific facility. Over the following month, the body and materials break down to form soil, which is delivered to loved ones for planting flowers, vegetables or trees. Advocates say there are multiple environmental benefits from the composting process, but also that it could resolve the issue of overcrowded cemeteries, particularly in metropolitan cities.

If you're a young person, chances are you're well across the rise in vapes – their use is widespread. According to the Cancer Council's public health chair in 2022, a 'public health crisis is rapidly unfolding before our eyes'. So, how harmful is vaping?

A 2023 study by Queensland's Health and Environment Committee of seventeen vape samples found that all the samples contained chemicals that can irritate lung tissue. In each, the committee found compounds typically used in the manufacturing of paint and refrigerants; five to fifteen types of heavy metals (including lead, mercury, nickel, aluminium, copper and iron); and all samples tested positive for nicotine. A number of the metals found are known to be carcinogenic.

A BIG QUESTION:

Are vapes harmful to your health?

This study is reinforced by one published in 2022 by researchers at ANU, who conducted a review of the global evidence on vaping, which found vaping caused 'significant harms'. The review noted evidence that it can lead to addiction, poisoning, seizures and lung injury; and that it could adversely affect blood pressure, heart rate, lung function and adolescent brain development. The latter effect is of particular concern to researchers: many vape manufacturers target their product specifically to young consumers, using colourful packaging, selling at relatively low price points, and promoting candy and fruit flavours. Some vapes also contain 'nicotine salt products', making higher concentrations of nicotine palatable to consumers.

The review found there remains a lack of evidence as to how vaping impacts a range of longer-term health conditions, including cardiovascular disease, cancer, mental health, child development, reproduction and sleep.

While we'll need to wait years before the longer-term impacts of vaping play out (it has been adopted on a substantive scale only since around the early 2010s), the federal government has already started to crack down on it. It has announced measures to restrict the flavours, colours and nicotine volumes for vapes, and plans to ban all single-use, disposable vapes.

According to Health Minister Mark Butler in 2023, 'Big Tobacco has taken another addictive product, wrapped it in shiny packaging and added flavours to create a new generation of nicotine addicts . . . This must end.'

But will it? We'll have to wait and see.

THE WOR[LD] AROU[ND] US

6.

.D
ND

WHY SHOULD I CARE ABOUT WORLD NEWS AND THE WORLD AROUND US?

The Daily Aus strives to cover both news that focuses on Australia and what's making headlines overseas.
   Perhaps it's due to Australia's smaller population, or the way Australians read the news, but international affairs are often front and centre of our news coverage.

Also top of our news agenda is Australia's place in the world – how we agree or disagree with policies and governments in other countries; whether we should form alliances with these countries or oppose them; whether we should trade with them; whether we should allow more citizens from other nations to migrate to Australia, or discourage it; where we import goods and services from, or if we steer our own manufacturing ship; whether we should chase our own climate goals or focus on pressuring other nations to pursue theirs.

This chapter is all about giving you some context for major world news stories and looking at Australia's place within them. We've tried to approach this from two angles: we'll look at Australia's international relationships (the dramatic ones, the stable ones and everything in between), and we'll check out the plotlines in which the nation doesn't play a key role but that are nonetheless important in order for us to understand the international stories that fill our newsfeeds.

When TDA reports on international affairs, we're curious to examine when and why a story becomes important to an Australian audience. How do we, as a news company, decide it is significant enough to bring it to our readers? If there's a natural disaster overseas, do we only start reporting on it when we discover Australians were involved? Even when a story is highly significant (say, the Russian invasion of Ukraine), should we be reporting on it every day for what could be a prolonged period?

This is a major challenge for us and all of Australia's media (and indeed every national media organisation in the world). We try to take a simple approach: is the event something our audience is talking about, and could do with some background to? Is it an issue TDA thinks our audience should know about?

It's a big world out there, so in this one chapter we simply aren't going to be able to cover everything we'd like to. The world is stricken by wars; intense political narratives unfold day-by-day in other nations; there are alternative models of governments; regularly, countries collaborate on groundbreaking and innovative projects.

With this in mind, here is an introduction to the major events of past years that have shaped world affairs and, therefore, also shaped Australia to differing degrees. First, however, let's get on top of some of the terms the media uses to describe foreign relations.

SCAN ME FOR MORE

YOUR FOREIGN POLICY PHRASEBOOK

What's the deal with . . . 'developed' and 'developing' nations?

Let's begin with two terms you've almost certainly heard before, but which we don't always stop to think about: developed and developing nations.

These terms split the countries of the world into two groups, based on their level of economic 'progress'. That progress is all about industrialisation. For much of history, humans have lived in agricultural societies, with little improvement in standard of living or life expectancy. This changed dramatically with the industrial revolution in the UK – the rise of factories and mass production, which would eventually lead to the advanced standard of living enjoyed in countries like Australia today.

'Developed' countries are those who have completed this transition. They typically perform highly on most measures of economic wellbeing and quality of life. 'Developing' countries are countries in the process of the transition.

Like any attempt to split the entire world into two halves, this distinction loses important nuance. For example, China is sometimes called a 'developing' country, and in some ways it fits the bill: it only began to transition from a predominantly agricultural society to an industrial one in the 1990s.

But China is also the world's second-largest country. The average Chinese citizen has an income more than fifty times higher than in Burundi, one of the poorest countries in the world, which is also classified as 'developing'.

There are large gaps between developed countries, too, although not quite as large: the average person in Norway has an income five times higher than the average person in Poland.

Of course, history explains a lot of the developed–developing divide: it is not a coincidence that many of the countries now classified as 'developing' were colonies of Britain and other European industrial powers. In fact, those European powers grew richer on the back of resources taken from their colonies, often at the expense of those same colonies.

THE WORLD BANK GOAL TO END EXTREME POVERTY BY 2030 IS NOT ON TRACK

The World Bank – an international institution whose mission statement is to 'reduce poverty and build shared prosperity in developing countries' – says the pandemic has been 'the biggest setback to global poverty-reduction efforts since [monitoring began in] 1990' and the war in Ukraine is likely to make the situation worse.[1]

Measuring poverty is not straightforward. Basically, it can be measured in an 'absolute' way, which means setting a global standard; for example, 'living on $2.15 a day is an indicator of poverty'. It can be measured in a 'relative' way, meaning compared to others in the same country (this is how we measure it in Australia). Those are financial measures. We can also measure non-financial poverty, such as ease of access to education or clean water. The World Bank uses a combination of these measures.

THE STAT

US$2.15
A DAY

Living on this amount (or less) is measure of extreme poverty

So, using that simple figure of US$2.15 a day, the World Bank estimates that at the end of 2020, 719 million people were in extreme poverty, and 600 million will remain in poverty by 2030. About 70 million were pushed into poverty in 2020 alone – the largest single-year increase since 1990.

The pandemic put pressure on health systems, led to many deaths and disrupted education due to school closures. In general, these factors were worse in developing countries. Also, it disrupted economic activity. Again, people in developing countries were hit harder, in part because their governments did not have the resources to provide financial support to mitigate the fallout.

CONTINUED NEXT PAGE →

> **CONTINUED**
>
> Before 2020, poverty was falling steadily. The World Bank believes progress started to slow in 2021 and 2022. The report suggests progress has slowed again because of higher prices for food and energy, driven by the war in Ukraine.
>
> What can be done? Well, the World Bank calls for global cooperation, and makes three recommendations for action at a national level.
>
> It advises countries with high rates of poverty to focus on cash transfers to the poor, not subsidies (e.g. for energy), since these are more likely to benefit the well-off. It suggests investing in education, research and infrastructure. It also recommends raising taxes on property or pollution, because these taxes are more likely to affect wealthier populations.

What's the deal with . . . the UN?

The United Nations was founded in the aftermath of World War II, stemming from a desire to ensure the horrific atrocities of two successive world wars could not be repeated.

Today, the UN is made up of 193 member states – plus two permanent non-member observer states, Palestine and Vatican City – who sign up to the principles contained in its founding charter. By joining the UN, a nation agrees to work to find peaceful solutions to international problems, provide aid for matters of international significance and be open to discussing concerns with other nations via peaceful dialogue.

When all 193 member states meet, they do so in the UN's General Assembly – a place for the world to gather to debate and vote on matters of global importance.

This might sound a little like a 'global parliament', and it does resemble that. However, there's one all-important difference: the UN cannot force member countries to do anything. Its only 'power' comes from its member states agreeing to abide by its rules and respect its resolutions. It maintains international 'laws' in the form of voluntary agreements and treaties between countries, but it can't enforce them in the same way a country can enforce its own laws. It's a global forum which only works if its participants 'play ball'.

This dynamic can be seen in the operation of the UN's many councils, most prominently the Human Rights Council and the

Security Council. Like their names suggest, these two councils focus on human rights and resolving conflicts. However, they only work if members respect their decisions. The Human Rights Council can declare a country has violated its human rights obligations but can't compel that country to change course. The Security Council has more teeth – it can authorise peacekeeping forces to intervene in a conflict – but any one of its five permanent members (the US, China, Russia, France and the UK) has the power to veto (block) any decision it disagrees with.

Still, the UN does a lot of vital humanitarian work around the world with the support of most or all of its members. For example, the UN World Food Programme provides food to people at risk of starvation, the UN Children's Fund (UNICEF) helps children in need and the UN Educational, Scientific and Cultural Organisation (UNESCO) preserves sites of cultural and natural significance.

What's the deal with . . . other major global organisations we report on?

Alongside the UN is a variety of other world bodies you will often see in our reporting. They can be a dizzying array of acronyms. Here are just a few.

First, there are three major global bodies for economic cooperation:

- **The WTO (World Trade Organization),** where countries meet to negotiate trade rules and settle trade-related disputes.
- **The World Bank,** which loans money to countries to aid their development.
- **The IMF (International Monetary Fund),** which loans money to governments in precarious financial positions, often requiring governments to make policy changes as a condition of receiving loans.

There are also a variety of significant global bodies which include a selection of countries rather than all of them. These are called multilateral organisations.

One of these is NATO (the North Atlantic Treaty Organization) – a military alliance between the US, Canada and several European countries. Australia isn't part of NATO, but is a 'key partner nation'. NATO has been in the news since the early 2020s because it has become a major supporter of Ukraine's defence against Russia's invasion. In fact, Ukraine had previously sought to join NATO, and although this has never eventuated, Russian president Vladimir Putin referenced Ukraine's wish to join NATO as a reason for the invasion, since Ukraine is its largest neighbour.

Another is the European Union (EU), a group of twenty-seven European countries who have agreed to hand over some economic and political decision-making power to a central body. The EU has its own parliament, and unlike the UN it can impose its decisions on EU members.

In Australia's region, there are several important forums designed to facilitate cooperation between neighbours, including APEC (the Asia-Pacific Economic Cooperation), APAC (A-sia PAC-ific), ASEAN (the Association of Southeast Asian Nations) and the recently formed IPEF (Indo-Pacific Economic Framework) – bodies that bring together collections of countries from our Indo-Pacific region. Australia is a member of all of these.

More recently, there has also been the introduction of the Quadrilateral Security Dialogue, or Quad. The Quad is an informal grouping designed to discuss shared interests in the Pacific and Indian Oceans. It includes the US, India, Japan and Australia.

Finally, we've got the 'Gs' – the G7 and G20. These are informal forums, which were originally established to facilitate economic cooperation but have merged into powerful bodies that discuss many issues of international significance.

The G7 is comprised of Canada, France, Germany, Italy, Japan, the UK and the US (the European Union is a 'non-enumerated' member).

The G20 includes the world's twenty largest economies: Argentina, Australia, Brazil, Canada, China, France, Germany, India, Indonesia, Italy, Japan, Republic of Korea, Mexico, Russia, Saudi Arabia, South Africa, Türkiye, the UK, the US and the EU.

In the news you'll mostly come across the Gs under two circumstances:

1. **THEY HOLD AN EMERGENCY MEETING** When a particular issue is so important for the global community that countries need to send representatives to these forums to reach urgent agreements. US president Joe Biden convened an emergency G7 (and NATO) meeting in 2022 when a rocket landed in Poland amid the Russian war on Ukraine.

2. **SUMMITS** These summits are regularly scheduled and can produce some pretty awesome staged photographs with coordinated outfits. There's something about a G20 class photo that's particularly awkward.

G7 AND G20

G7

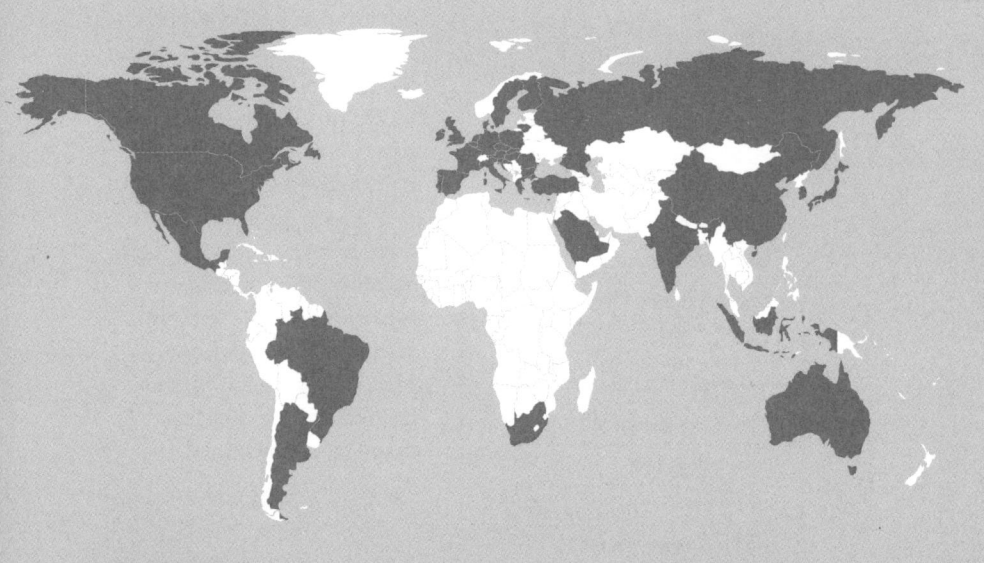

G20

What's the deal with... nuclear weapons?

The rather terrifying topic of nuclear weapons finds its way into many of our discussions on international affairs. Nuclear bombs have only been used militarily twice, when the US attacked Japan at the end of World War II, killing hundreds of thousands of civilians in the cities of Hiroshima and Nagasaki, both in the immediate blast and through the poisonous effects of radiation in the weeks, months and years following.[2]

Their devastating and long-term impacts are understood by the world's governments to be far worse than any military gains achieved by their detonation, which is why most of the UN's member countries have signed the Treaty on the Non-Proliferation of Nuclear Weapons, and those who have nuclear weapons have stated a commitment to reducing the size of their stockpiles.

Nuclear bombs are made with radioactive material – uranium and its extract, plutonium – which damages or kills our cells, causing aggressive cancers and DNA mutations. The explosion of a nuclear bomb sprays radioactive material in a huge area around the point of impact, blowing it upwards into the sky in a mushroom cloud and dispersing it through the air, water and ground. It wouldn't be possible, therefore, to limit the effect of a nuclear bomb to just one country – the fallout would be widely spread, and the impact on the global food supply from nuclear clouds blocking the sun and radioactive material mutating the cells of every living thing would be devastating.

There are still many nuclear weapons in the world in many different countries. Australia is officially a non-nuclear state, but many of our allies, including the US and the UK, do have arsenals of different kinds of nuclear weapons.

THE COUNTRIES THAT (WE KNOW) HAVE NUCLEAR WEAPONS

Country	Approximate number
Russia	about 6000
US	about 5400
China	about 350
France	about 300
India	about 150
Pakistan	about 150
UK	about 120
Israel	about 100
North Korea	about 30

THE TWENTY-FIRST CENTURY: (A CURATED LIST OF) TWELVE DAYS THAT HAVE SHAPED OUR WORLD

9 NOVEMBER 1989
FALL OF THE BERLIN WALL

Okay, we're probably not starting this list on the best note because we're technically cheating here (1989 is obviously not in the twenty-first century). But if there's one day from the twentieth century that helps to explain today's world, it's this one.

The second half of the twentieth century was shaped by the Cold War between the US, the Soviet Union and their respective allies. It was called a 'cold' war because there was no direct fighting, but the threat of war (including nuclear weapons) loomed large for decades.

The conflict was framed as a struggle between American capitalism and Russian communism. The German city of Berlin, which had been divided up between the two powers after World War II (by a literal wall), came to symbolise this struggle.

The fall of that wall was the beginning of the end for Russian communism and was followed in 1991 by the collapse of the Soviet Union.

11 SEPTEMBER 2001
THE 9/11 TERROR ATTACKS

The end of the Cold War brought with it a sense of confidence and triumph for the US. This was shaken on September 11, 2001, when nineteen hijackers killed nearly 3000 people after crashing three planes into the two towers of the World Trade Center in New York City, and the Pentagon in Virginia. Another plane, headed for Washington DC, crashed in a field in Pennsylvania after passengers and crew struggled to regain control of it mid-air. Al-Qaeda – a militant Islamist extremist network – claimed responsibility for the attacks.

20 MARCH 2003
THE WAR IN IRAQ

On this day, the US, UK, Australia and other allies began a coordinated invasion of Iraq, citing evidence that the nation was not only connected to 9/11 but also possessed weapons of mass destruction – and that the dictatorial rule of its president, Saddam Hussein, needed to be overturned. No weapons of mass destruction were ever found.

20 JANUARY 2008
INAUGURATION OF PRESIDENT BARACK OBAMA

For the first time in US history, an African American person held the highest office in the country and one of the most important jobs in the world. President Obama's swearing-in to office had one in three televisions in the US tuning in. Obama ran on a campaign of optimism – 'Hope' and 'Yes We Can' became synonymous with the president, who went on to lead for two full terms.

15 SEPTEMBER 2008
THE GLOBAL FINANCIAL CRISIS (GFC)

It's hard to pinpoint one day in 2008 that encapsulates the GFC, but the collapse of Lehman Brothers – a major US financial services firm, and then the fourth-biggest investment bank in the country – was a pivotal point. Lehman's remains the largest bankruptcy filing in US history, involving more than US$600 billion (yep, that's billion with a b) in assets and 25,000 immediately redundant employees. The reason for the crash? Lehman, like most of the global financial system, had filled its books with US home loans that were not as solid as they looked – often, the loans had been made to people with no income, no jobs and no real chance of repaying them. Home loans of this kind had spread around the global financial system, so Lehman's collapse (and that of other financial institutions) triggered global panic. Australia was not immune to the fallout, but was one of the few developed countries that did not enter a recession.

18 DECEMBER
2010
THE ARAB SPRING

In the Middle East and North Africa, the end of 2010 and the first few months of 2011 were filled with protests against a number of longstanding authoritarian regimes. Tunisia and Egypt were the first scenes of widespread public marches, which were soon emulated in Yemen, Bahrain, Libya, Syria, Algeria, Jordan, Morocco and Oman. Not every country was changed by the demonstrations – horrible scenes of violent crackdowns by security forces were disseminated online throughout the early months of 2010. The Arab Spring was one of the first major world events to be blogged, posted and livestreamed.

14 MARCH
2013
XI JINPING BECOMES PRESIDENT OF CHINA

When former vice president Xi was appointed president of China by the Chinese Communist Party, little was known about what type of leader he would become. However, under Xi China's economy has continued to expand, while the government has increased both its surveillance of its own citizens and its military capacity at the fastest rate of any country since World War II. In 2018, Xi changed the rules that had limited presidents to two five-year terms in office, effectively paving the way for him to be president for life.

27 FEBRUARY
2014
THE ANNEXATION OF CRIMEA

Crimea is a small territory situated between Russia and Ukraine, and was seized by Russia in the early months of 2014. Russian president Vladimir Putin justified the annexation (which means taking possession of territory to add to an existing, neighbouring territory) by claiming he was both protecting land that Russia had a historical claim over and neutralising threats against Crimeans from 'far-right extremists' in Ukraine.

8 NOVEMBER
2016
ELECTION OF PRESIDENT TRUMP

Amid chaotic presidential debates, campaign speeches at sold-out stadiums and a war of words on social media channels, the 2016 US presidential election was possibly one of the most highly charged in modern history. While some polling models gave Democratic candidate Hillary Clinton a 90 per cent chance of winning, it was Republican Donald Trump who stormed home in several key swing states (he was the first Republican since 1984 to win in Wisconsin, for example). Trump's turbulent presidency fundamentally changed politics, the US and the way we think about political polling.

1 OCTOBER
2019
THE HONG KONG PROTESTS

On the seventieth anniversary of the establishment of the People's Republic of China, anti-government protests in Hong Kong turned deadly when police began to fire live rounds of ammunition on protestors (in the months before, they had used rubber bullets). Chinese president Xi Jinping's vision of 'national unity' – a unified China and Hong Kong – was being challenged on the streets, particularly directly at lawmakers who proposed a plan to allow extradition (the deportation of a prisoner) to mainland China from Hong Kong. Those in Hong Kong feared this would endanger free speech and political opposition – and while the bill was withdrawn in September, demonstrations continued through the rest of the year.

15 MARCH 2020

COVID-19

In January 2020, the world began to learn about a disease believed to have originated in the seafood wet market of Wuhan, China. On this day in March, Australia's first National Cabinet meeting was held, and ruled that anyone entering Australia was required to self-isolate for fourteen days. By 18 March, non-essential indoor gatherings of more than a hundred people were banned, and the official travel advice issued to all Australians was simple: 'Do not travel.' From there . . . well, we're pretty sure we don't need to remind you.

24 FEBRUARY 2022

THE RUSSIAN INVASION OF UKRAINE

After weeks of escalating fears about Russia gathering masses of troops on the Russia–Ukraine border, president Vladimir Putin authorised what he called a 'special military operation' in Ukraine, ordering his forces to commence a missile and artillery attack on a number of Ukrainian cities, including the capital, Kyiv. Ukraine's president Volodymyr Zelenskyy, using a combination of state broadcasts and social media channels such as Telegram, declared martial law (the suspension of 'normal law' by a government to mobilise a country in a conflict). When the US offered Zelenskyy an evacuation so he could lead the country from a safe distance, he replied, 'The fight is here; I need ammunition, not a ride.'

AUSTRALIA AND CHINA

We've finished our whirlwind tour of the world, its key institutions and key events. Time to go back home and take a closer look at Australia's relationships with the key players. First: China.

Australia and China have a complicated relationship. Here's the TL;DR: Australia has profited enormously from its economic relationship with China, especially China's purchase of iron ore (one of our largest exports). China remains our largest trading partner.

On the other hand, China's global posture has shifted in recent years. This has included threatening or imposing economic penalties on countries who criticise its human rights policies, including Australia.

Let's take a step back. In World War II, China, led by the Nationalist Party of China (NCP), was a western ally. But in 1949, the Chinese Communist Party (CCP) took over, led by Mao Zedong and allied to the Soviet Union for much of the Cold War. Most of the west, including Australia, did not recognise the CCP's authority, instead continuing to recognise the NCP, who had fled to the island of Taiwan, off the coastline of mainland China.

Then, in December 1972, Australian prime minister Gough Whitlam officially recognised the People's Republic of China, something Whitlam had agitated for since the mid-1950s. The US government made a similar move at a similar time. As part of this process, Australia recognised Taiwan as a province of China and not a country in itself, and removed its diplomats from Taiwan (put a pin in this – more to come).

By January 1973, Australia had set up its first embassy in Beijing and established trade relations, and later that year Whitlam became the first Australian PM to visit China, as well as signing a trade agreement, which still exists, with its government.

The economic relationship became an important one, and by the early 2000s it was common for Australian politicians to refer to China as a 'great friend'.

However, the relationship became more strained as Australia began to speak out about a wide range of human rights issues in China under President Xi, including China's treatment of political prisoners and ethnic minorities (including alleged crimes against humanity against the Uyghur ethnic minority), torture, the death penalty, and the rights of legal practitioners and civil rights activists.

Things got tense. In 2020, China issued an 'extraordinary attack on the Australian government' via the deliberate release of documents that accused Australia of 'poisoning bilateral relations'.[3] Then, China ordered all Australian journalists to leave the country, and as of 2023 hardly any can report there.

In an economic context, recent diplomatic tensions between the two nations have led to tariffs and trade blocks by China. Since 2020, there's been an effort to repair relations, but both countries are treading extremely carefully.

Help me understand Taiwan

There's been a long history of territorial tension between Taiwan and China since Taiwan split from China in 1949. Essentially, Taiwan runs itself as a sovereign state (independent from any other power), while China views Taiwan as one of its provinces – it often says China's 'reunification' with Taiwan 'must be fulfilled' and it claims it has the right to use military force to do this.

In a speech in Canberra in August 2022, China's ambassador to Australia said China considered Taiwan as much a part of China as Tasmania is considered part of Australia. President Xi promised to realise 'peaceful reunification'. He added that 'no one should underestimate the Chinese people's strong determination, will and capability to safeguard national sovereignty and territorial integrity'.

Following that statement, Taiwan's president Tsai Ing-wen said, 'We will do our utmost to prevent the status quo from being unilaterally altered. We will continue to bolster our national defence and demonstrate our determination to defend ourselves in order to ensure that nobody can force Taiwan to take the path China has laid out for us.'

Okay, so what is the 'One China' policy?

Taiwan's government is only recognised by some countries, due to Beijing's 'One China' policy, which is the diplomatic acknowledgement by the US, Australia and many others of China's territorial claim over Taiwan. It extends to not recognising Taiwan as an independent country. Adherence to the policy is notoriously ambiguous: while the US officially states that it 'does not support Taiwan's independence', it also says 'maintaining strong, unofficial relations with Taiwan is a major US goal'. Australia also emphasises its intention to maintain unofficial ties with Taiwan.

In August 2022, Nancy Pelosi, then the Speaker of the US House of Representatives – which made her the political and parliamentary leader of the Lower House, and second in line to the president after the vice president – visited Taiwan, because, she said, 'Beijing has dramatically intensified tensions with Taiwan' and their 'robust democracy . . . is under threat'.

This was a big moment in international relations. Unsurprisingly, the Chinese government firmly opposed the visit, viewing it as an 'external interference' that could promote Taiwan's independence.

During the visit, China held a number of military drills in the airspace and seas near Taiwan, in a perceived show of strength while the world was watching. At the time, Taiwan's foreign minister, Joseph Wu, said, 'China has used the drills in its military playbook to prepare for invasion of Taiwan.'

In the month after the visit, in an interview on US television, President Biden said that US forces would defend Taiwan 'if there was an unprecedented attack' on the island by China. Biden confirmed that by 'defend' he meant US troops entering Taiwan, a step further than the support of equipment and financing the US has provided Ukraine in its war against Russia.

Where does Australia fit in to all of this?

Australian governments (on both sides of politics) advocate for restraint and de-escalation in any conflicts over Taiwan. Australia has maintained its support for the 'One China' policy, while at the same time backing Taiwan's participation in international organisations 'where appropriate'. The government says it 'strongly supports the development, on an unofficial basis, of economic and cultural relations with Taiwan'.

AUSTRALIA AND THE PACIFIC

Let's move now to the Pacific, where we are connected to nations due to a number of issues, mainly China's rising influence and the effects of the climate crisis.

Securing trade, economic and cultural ties with our Pacific neighbours has been a focus of Australia's foreign policy since 2000. In the past five years or so especially, Australia has grappled with its role as one of the most developed – and powerful – nations in the region, and with our moral responsibilities to assist in the development and security of less well-off countries around us.

Papua New Guinea is a significant nation in the Pacific region, and one that historically has had close ties to Australia, so let's look first at this relationship.

In December 2021, Australia provided PNG with a $650 million loan to help meet its 2021 budget financing shortfall, assist with the ongoing health and economic impact of the COVID-19 pandemic, and continue its progress on economic reforms under the International Monetary Fund Staff-Monitored Program. In total, Australia has provided PNG with approximately $1.2 billion in budget support since 2019.

Of the Pacific countries, Aotearoa New Zealand is one of our closest cultural and geographic neighbours. We collaborate on strategic decisions in the region and have a long history of military cooperation. Australia has had a free-trade agreement with New Zealand since the early 1980s.

In 2021, Pacific neighbour Solomon Islands signed a security agreement with China. Solomon Islands is 2000 kilometres north-east of Australia. At the time of the signing, the Australian government expressed concern that closer cooperation between China and Solomon Islands could pose a long-term threat, especially if it were to lead to a Chinese military base in the country.

After the Albanese government won the 2022 election, Foreign Minister Penny Wong visited Solomon Islands, and said she 'welcomed an assurance that Australia remains Solomon Islands' first security partner of choice and first development partner of choice'.[4]

SPEED-DATING SUPERPOWERS: RISING ASIAN POWERHOUSE NATIONS IN THREE STATS

Japan

1. Japan has the world's third-largest economy – and most of its economic growth has occurred in the second half of the twentieth century.
2. It faces a rapidly ageing population – 15 per cent of the population is aged over 75 (about 20 million people). By 2030, one in five Japanese citizens will be over 75. Life expectancy is 84 – up from 72 in 1970.
3. It's expected Japan's ageing population could lower its GDP by 1 per cent a year in the years leading to 2050.

World's third-largest economy

Ageing population

India

1. By 2032, India's population will overtake China's to become the world's largest, peaking at 1.7 billion in the 2060s.
2. India's GDP has multiplied by five times since 1970. It's grown every year for thirty-five years.
3. The share of India's population living in poverty has fallen sharply – 415 million people have been lifted out of poverty since 2007.

World's largest population by 2032

Poverty fallen sharply

Indonesia

1. Indonesia is the world's third-largest democracy, with the world's largest Muslim population.
2. Economic forecasters predict that Indonesia will become a top-five global economy by 2050.
3. The four richest billionaires in Indonesia have more wealth than the poorest 40 per cent of the population – that's about 100 million people.

> World's third-largest democracy

> Top-five global economy by 2050

Vietnam

1. Vietnam has the highest economic growth projection of any east or south-east Asian nation at 7.2 per cent.
2. Foreign direct investment (mostly multinational companies setting up manufacturing operations) has grown over 200 times since 1986, and it's not slowing down. Vietnam's exports increased by 19 per cent in a single year during the pandemic.
3. Vietnam has experienced sharp economic and population growth – and its infrastructure can't keep up. The country ranks 47th of 160 in the World Bank's infrastructure rankings, and 103rd in road quality.

> Foreign direct investment growth

> Ranked 47 for infrastructure by World Bank

AUSTRALIA, THE US AND THE UK

The relationship between Australia, the US and the UK has historically been fairly straightforward. The three nations fought on the same side of both world wars and have retained extremely close ties since. In a 2023 Defence Strategic review, the Australian government made clear that 'close cooperation with the United States is central to achieving balance and stability in the Indo-Pacific'.

THE EU AND BREXIT

WHAT IS BREXIT? One event that monumentally shaped the way not only Australia, but every country in the world, dealt with the UK was 'Brexit'.

In 2016 the then-prime minister of Britain, David Cameron, called for a referendum in the UK that asked 'Should the United Kingdom remain a member of the European Union or leave the European Union?' After a hard-fought campaign, the country voted to leave the EU by a vote of 52 to 48 per cent. The results differed dramatically in age groups, with the majority of those over 45 voting 'Leave', and 73 per cent of those aged 18 to 24 voting 'Remain'.[5]

WHY DID BRITAIN WANT TO LEAVE? The 'Leave' campaign argued that the EU's economic policies – including product standards and regulations – were constraining the UK's own sovereign power. The campaign also linked membership of the EU to what they framed as uncontrolled immigration, since the EU allows free movement between all EU members.[6]

HOW DID THE COUNTRY ACTUALLY LEAVE THE EU? After years of negotiation, failed bills in the British Parliament, and two prime ministers resigning as a result of the vote (Cameron) and of being unable to extricate the UK from the EU (Theresa May), the UK finally left in early 2020.

Why was leaving so complicated? The UK was trying to negotiate new trade rules to replace the previous free trade it had agreed to with other EU members. A particular challenge was how to resolve the border between Northern Ireland (part of the UK) and Ireland (a separate country and an EU member). This issue was only resolved in 2023 with a series of special concessions that would prevent a 'hard border' between Northern Ireland and Ireland.

In 2021, Australia and the US, alongside the UK, announced the formation of AUKUS – a trilateral (three-country) security agreement to confirm cooperation on defence strategy, intelligence and the stability of the Pacific region.

This arrangement will see Australia secure nuclear-powered submarines using highly secretive US technology. You might recall that in 2021 this got Scott Morrison's government into some hot water with France, with whom Australia had a pre-existing contract to build (non-nuclear-powered) submarines. Morrison dropped the $90 billion contract with France in favour of US-made submarines, prompting French president Emmanuel Macron to tell journalists that Morrison had lied to him.[7] Drama!

AUSTRALIA AND THE MIDDLE EAST

In the coming decades, the Middle East will be a hub of increasing economic activity, tourism and innovation. A great deal of trade is also conducted in the region, some of which has been a bridge for its divided nations, with the United Arab Emirates and Israel signing an historic, multi-billion-dollar trade agreement in 2022.

The region is also vitally important because of the wealth of its resources – oil and gas. Around a third of the world's total oil reserves are in the Middle East.

Australia has maintained a military presence in the Middle East for almost eighty of the past one hundred years, and our defence policy has continually had to consider the implications of turbulence in the region.[8]

At the time of writing, there are more Australian defence operations underway in the Middle East region than any other part of the world. However, Australia's military presence has significantly lessened as our strategic focus has turned to the Indo-Pacific, and especially following the withdrawal from Afghanistan.

Afghanistan: Australia's withdrawal from Kabul

In June 2021, Australia's two-decades-long military deployment to Afghanistan quietly concluded when the last Australian troops were sent home. This drawdown represented the final part of Australia's role in the US-led global war on terror that had been the focus of Australia's defence force's operational attention for the previous twenty years.

Let's go back a bit. Between the end of 2001, after 9/11, and the first half of 2021, the US was at war with the Taliban. The Taliban (a Pashto word that means 'students') emerged as an Islamist movement in the early 1990s, with its roots in northern Pakistan. Following 9/11, the US accused it of providing refuge to Osama bin Laden and Al-Qaeda. By December 2001, US troops had removed the Taliban from power in Afghanistan.

Over the next two decades, US-led coalition forces attempted to stabilise the region and train Afghan security forces for an eventual handover. However, simultaneous military campaigns in both Afghanistan and Iraq spread resources thin, allowing the Taliban to rebuild their forces.

When the US, UK and Australia started to withdraw troops from key areas of the country in May 2021, the Taliban stepped up its offensive campaign. By August they had taken Kabul and were back in power. Fears that they would bring back hardline rule proved correct as they swept aside reforms, including pushing women out of schools, universities and public life. Rina Amiri, the US Special Envoy for Afghan Women, Girls and Human Rights, said:

> When I talk to women . . . what I hear is devastation over the situation and that they've lost the right to work, they've lost the right to get their daughters educated, they have lost any sense of hope for the future. And for ethnic and religious communities, what they note is that they live under the shadow of threat.[9]

There's another layer to this. Many Afghan citizens played pivotal roles in Australia's operations in Afghanistan during the war, acting as local guides, translators, colleagues and friends. In August 2021, those people suddenly faced Taliban power with little protection. The scenes at Kabul Airport that are seared into the world's collective conscience remind us of the terror, desperation and chaos of so many who, despite their work for Australia and a number of other Western nations, now had nowhere to turn. Many sought out Australia. Between the time the Taliban seized control and the end of 2022, there were 177,000 applications from Afghans seeking an Australian visa. It's unclear how many have been granted as of mid-2023, but we do know that the federal government has allocated 31,500 permanent visa places for Afghans from 2021 until 2026.

AUSTRALIA AND EASTERN EUROPE

It is all but impossible to finish a chapter about the world around us without talking about Russia's invasion of Ukraine. We've referenced the war throughout this book, but what does Australia's relationship with this whole region currently look like?

The first key thing to note is that Australia has, like its allies, clearly supported Ukraine in this conflict. There have been many speeches by both the Coalition and Labor governments declaring support for Ukraine. Australia has also provided ongoing financial support to Ukraine's army to increase its defence capabilities. This funding does not mean that Australia has sent troops to Ukraine – it hasn't. Instead, it has sought to provide funding to increase Ukrainians' local capacity through various measures. Australia has also allocated funding for humanitarian assistance to the Ukrainian people and is prioritising visa applications for Ukrainian nationals.

On the flipside, Australia has, alongside key Western allies, sought to diminish the power of Russia by banning imports of Russian oil, petrol and gas, and imposing broad financial sanctions on the country.

The ramifications of this war have been wide-ranging, with the humanitarian, economic and diplomatic consequences shaping the world around us.

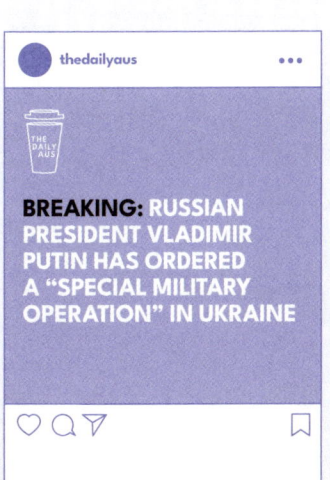

In the past five y[ears] especially, Aust[ralia has] grappled with it[s role as one] of the most dev[eloped, and] powerful – natio[ns in our] region, and with [its] **responsibilities** the developmen[t] of less well-off [nations] around us.

ars or so
lia has
role as one
oped – and
 in the Pacific
our moral
 assist in
nd security
untries

THE BRIGHT SIDE

1
CHILD MORTALITY HAS HIT AN ALL-TIME LOW.

The world has made substantial progress on lowering rates of child mortality. A century ago, every third child aged five or under died. Almost a century later the child-mortality rate has fallen to 4 per cent. This progress has been substantial in recent decades. In 2020, 1 in 27 children died before reaching age five, compared to 1 in 11 children in 1990.

Look, we'll be honest. Learning about international affairs can be a confronting experience, because of the complexity of . . . well, the world. Where there are people, there may always be conflict, disadvantage and injustice.

But, against that backdrop, the wins must be noted. As the founder of Our World in Data, Max Roser, notes, 'The world is awful. The world is much better. The world can be much better. All three statements are true at the same time.'[10]

Here's what the data tells us about how the world is doing 'much better' (noting, of course, the world can be 'much better' again).

2
WE'RE LIVING LONGER.

Since the 1900s, the global average life expectancy has more than doubled. Both female and male life expectancy have increased in the last three decades, with the greatest gains in Africa and Asia.[11]

3
POLIO COULD SOON BE ERADICATED GLOBALLY.

Polio is an infectious disease contracted primarily by children, which can invade the nervous system and cause paralysis. In 1998, the Global Polio Eradication Initiative was launched with the aim to eradicate polio worldwide. Since then, polio cases have decreased by more than 99 per cent. In 2021 the virus was found to circulate in only two countries in the world.

And so, while progress isn't always linear, fast or clear, it is happening. The world and our lives in it are, albeit slowly, improving on several key indicators. While there is much to rue about the state of international affairs, it is through international collaboration and cooperation that we are moving forward as a society.

A BIG QUESTION:

Should you be able to erase all your online personal data?

When the federal government published the recommendations of a review into Australia's privacy laws, there were some that caught TDA's eye. Notably, those to cement a legal right to object to the collection of information, to opt out of targeted ads, and to erase personal information online.

The right to privacy in Australia is protected by the *Privacy Act 1988*, and while it has been updated since, lawmakers have been slow to adapt it to online privacy risks. In 2020, however, the Coalition government commissioned a review to consider how to make it fit for purpose now.

One recommendation was to broaden the types of personal information covered by existing legal privacy rights, including specifying legal protection for IP addresses or geolocation data, which can be used to identify you. It also includes protections for 'inferred' information – the stuff a website learns about you even though you're not actively providing it. We're looking at you, random ads for hammocks after we searched 'tropical getaway' once.

And here's where things get juicy – a range of new rights were recommended, including the right to object to the collection or use of personal information. That means you telling a website or service that you don't want them to remember you engaged with them (but first you must find the sneaky 'Do Not Track' button in your browser). Also, the right to erase, correct or 'de-index' from search engines any online personal information; to request information a website has collected on you; and to opt out of direct marketing and targeted advertising.

This is, in other jurisdictions, known as the 'right to be forgotten'. It is codified into law in Türkiye, the Philippines and the European Union, and was recognised by the European Court of Justice as a right of all people. Today, the online content in question could be an embarrassing Facebook post you're tagged in, a photo posted in a forum that you'd rather forget, or (for the more famous among us) a piece of salacious gossip you want to disappear.

Critics of this law argue that the ability to remove information from the internet is a threat to freedom of expression, and have compared it to being able to march into a library to demand certain books or journals be pulped. At one end of the spectrum, businesses could use the law to delete references to bad behaviour on their part (for example, a restaurant might ask for negative, but accurate, reviews to be taken down) and at the other, more serious end, individuals could erase references to and evidence of past criminality that may predict future behaviours. Of course, the counter-argument is that a bad review of a restaurant might be untrue or unfair and ruin a good business, or a reformed criminal may never be able to escape past misdemeanours.

Currently, it's up to the tech giants to facilitate ways for individuals to request data be deleted or removed – and agree to the requests. But, without any law to enforce, it's totally up to them to decide whether your claim is worthy.

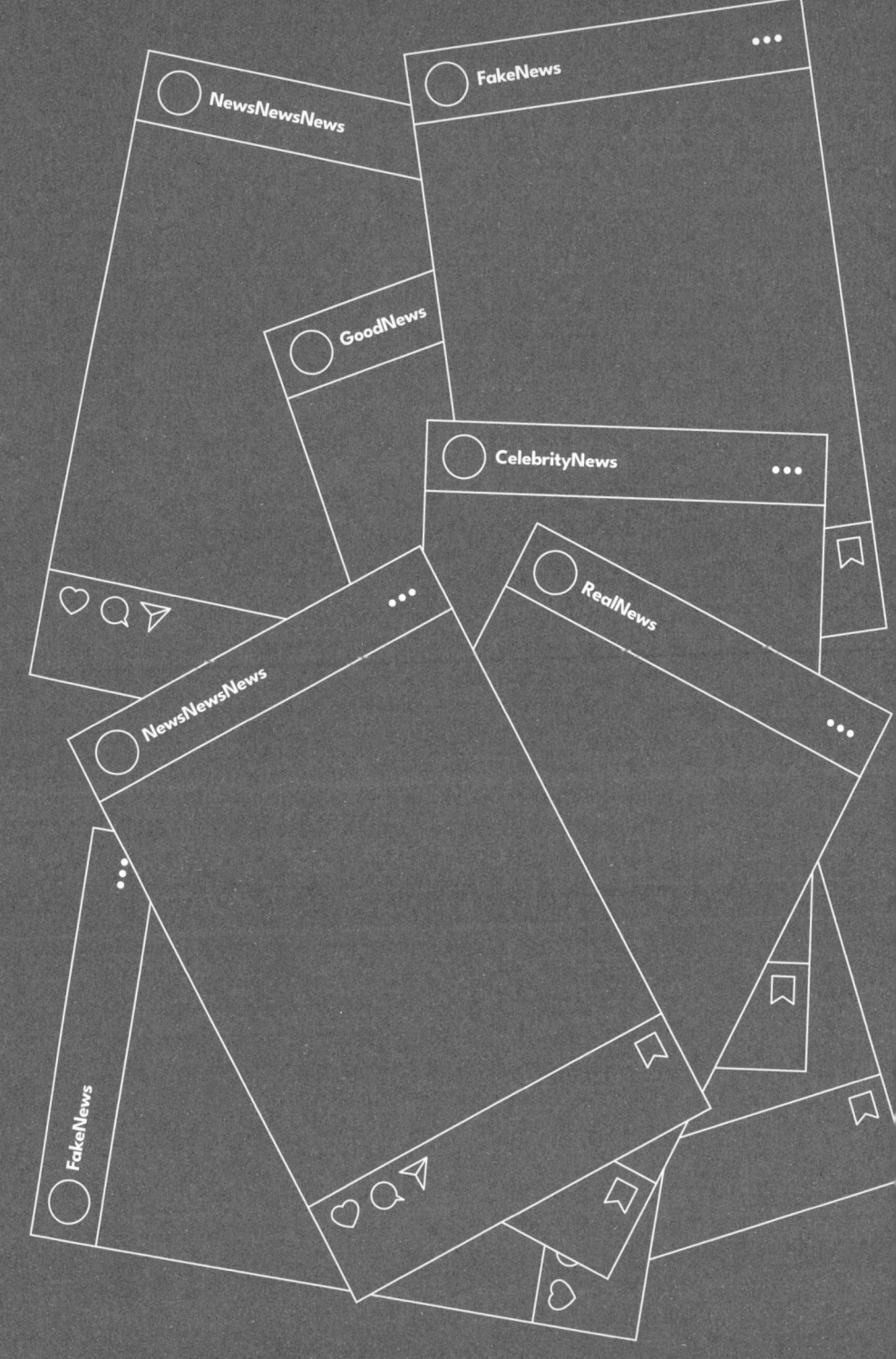

CONCLUSION: HOW TO READ THE NEWS

All right – you're armed with your starter pack for understanding the world. You know how preferential voting works, how inflation works, what net zero is and what happened when the Berlin Wall fell. So, you're ready to understand all the news that exists out there . . . right? Right?!

Not entirely.

There's one thing left to cover, and that's how to be a critical news reader.

No, that doesn't mean criticising news companies (although that can be part of it!). It means developing the ability to interrogate the news yourself, asking and answering questions like: why has this article been presented the way it has? How do I know if what I'm reading is true? Is it missing important context?

Put simply, being a critical news reader is about media literacy.

As the co-founders of a media company, it may not surprise you to know we care a lot about media literacy. In fact, it's probably the subject in this book we are most passionate about. So, we wanted to end by outlining just a few tools we think are useful for navigating the news.

First, though, a word of apology on behalf of our profession: you will notice that a lot of these tips for you are actually warnings about things the media often does badly: bias, sensationalism and misinformation. As a media company, avoiding those things is first and foremost our responsibility, not yours. But knowledge is power, and we think an audience that's better at spotting bad coverage will be better placed to hold the media to account. So, think of this list as a how-to guide for keeping us accountable.

1. BEWARE OF CLICKBAIT

You know clickbait when you see it ('You'll never believe what the prime minister has been hiding from us all'). It's a headline with the sole purpose, as the name suggests, of grabbing your attention and making sure you click a link to a particular page. What is this famous person hiding from us? We're intrigued!

The problem with clickbait is that the headline is usually sensationalised to 'bait' you into reading a story that, in reality, is fairly different to the headline. Turns out the prime minister is 'hiding' that he is travelling to the UK for a pre-planned diplomatic trip. Nothing out of the ordinary; equally, nothing particularly unbelievable to read about.

Our advice? Never read only the headline. To fully understand a story, you need to read it in its entirety.

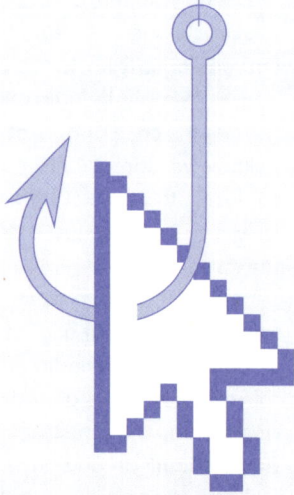

2.
POLITICAL BIAS

This one is a can of worms: debates about bias are some of the most heated among media watchers.

The definition is fairly simple: a publication is biased if its coverage favours or pushes a particular political view.

However, identifying bias can be tricky in practice. For example, many newspapers have a consistent political leaning in their opinion section, and this is usually easy to spot. But identifying whether this bias also affects the way these outlets cover factual news can be more difficult. There isn't a cheat code here – sadly, news outlets don't put up a useful sign on their home pages declaring their biases.

One strategy is to take media ownership into consideration. Media owners can exert influence over the leanings of their publications directly (by telling their editors and journalists what to do) or indirectly (by hiring people who have similar views to them).

In Australia, two corporations and interconnected entities own much of the country's media: Nine Entertainment and News Corp Australia. The owner of News Corp, Rupert Murdoch, is such a controversial figure that two former Australian prime ministers from opposite sides of politics have called for a royal commission into the apparent bias of his many media outlets.

But beyond this obvious example, you are your own best guide: as you become more familiar with reading stories from different outlets, it'll soon become clear which outlets skew towards the left and right of the political spectrum on different issues. Sometimes you might find it useful to hear reporting with such a clearly defined perspective and leaning, but whether you do or not, it never hurts to be aware of the opinions across the spectrum so you're reading with your eyes open.

3. FALSE BALANCE OR 'BOTHSIDESISM'

What's the opposite of biased journalism? Many people would answer 'balanced journalism'. Balance is an important part of journalism, but it has its own pitfalls. In particular, news outlets often fall into the trap of presenting two opposing perspectives on an issue as if they were equally valid, even when one of the perspectives is supported by evidence and the other is not. This can create a false impression of a debate and make ill-informed positions seem more legitimate than they are.

For example, a report by Northwestern University found that 'bothsidesism' in journalism is making it harder to address climate change. One of the researchers on the study, David Rapp, put it this way:

> Climate change is a great case study of the false balance problem, because the scientific consensus is nearly unanimous. If 99 doctors said you needed surgery to save your life, but one disagreed, chances are you'd listen to the 99 . . . But we often see one climate scientist pitted against one climate denier or down-player, as if it's a 50–50 split.[1]

How can you combat false balance in the media? Consume a variety of media! If you care about an issue, the more you read about it, the more you'll learn. You'll quickly develop a better ability to tell whether media outlets are presenting a story fairly or not.

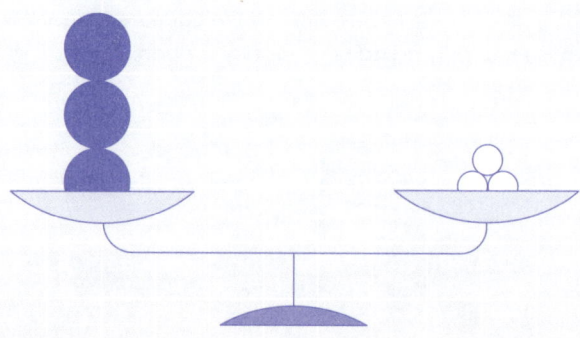

4.
THE ALGORITHM

Of course, it's not just media outlets who have biases. We all do (whether we are aware of them or not), and they impact the way we consume news. These biases overlap and interact in many ways, and all of them are heightened by social media's best friend, the algorithm.

If you get your news from social media, you're likely to be served the content you most interact with, therefore creating a vicious cycle of confirmation bias. The stuff you care about the most gets fed back to you, over and over again, while the stuff you don't interact with as often may never come across your screen.

A direct result of this is that you can end up in an echo chamber – whether that be online or in real life. An echo chamber occurs when you only encounter beliefs or opinions that match your own. You might not realise that you're in one, especially if we're talking about real-life examples where you're hanging out with people because you have similar values. But echo chambers can be dangerous, especially when there's a refusal to engage willingly with other sides of the debate.

One good way to ensure you're not confined to an echo chamber is by actively going out of your comfort zone to engage with and consume media that doesn't necessarily align with your beliefs – it means you're across different perspectives and approaches.

5.
MISINFORMATION AND DISINFORMATION

Fun fact: misinformation and disinformation mean different things!

Both refer to information that is misleading, erroneous or false, and which can cause harm. The difference is intent: misinformation can be shared and created by people who are unaware that it's inaccurate; disinformation is spread with the intent of causing harm. This means the terms can potentially apply to the same claim.

Let's use as an example Donald Trump's false claim that the result of the 2020 US presidential election was illegitimate. If your great-aunt shared this claim on Facebook, there's a decent chance she was misinformed, and was spreading that misinformation.

However, it's generally agreed that Trump and his allies spread the claim deliberately even though they knew it was false. Their decision to do so was disinformation.

Once again, there's no cheat code for recognising misinformation or disinformation. Your nose is probably your best guide – if a claim smells fishy, it might be. It might be possible for you to fact-check it yourself by searching for the source of the claim – has it come from a legitimate, official source such as a government website, or another reputable one such as a well-known university or a qualified expert?

Of course, you won't always have time for this. That's why it's important to seek out media organisations you trust. But just like in any relationship, trust is something that has to be earnt. Earning the trust of our readers is without question the most important part of our work at The Daily Aus. For us, it starts with being transparent about where our information comes from.

6.

IS SOMEONE PAYING FOR THIS?

One thing to keep in mind, especially as digital media continues to expand and transform, is the prevalence of something we call 'native advertising'.

Imagine this: you're really keen to check out the newest bar in Brisbane's CBD, so you type into Google 'best bars in Brisbane's CBD'. You click on the first result, which is a list curated by a cool, youth-oriented publisher. It looks like a normal editorial piece, it reads like a normal editorial piece . . . but at the very bottom of the article is an unobtrusive disclaimer. It explains that the number one bar on the list you've just read paid for the list to be created.

From our experience, brands are definitely pushing for more of this type of advertising, and less of the overt advertising you might get before a YouTube video or on free-to-air television. While it's on regulators and publishers to make sure the industry is sticking to the rules about declaring paid-for content, as a consumer it is always good to keep an eye out for disclaimers and consider how they may impact editorial output.

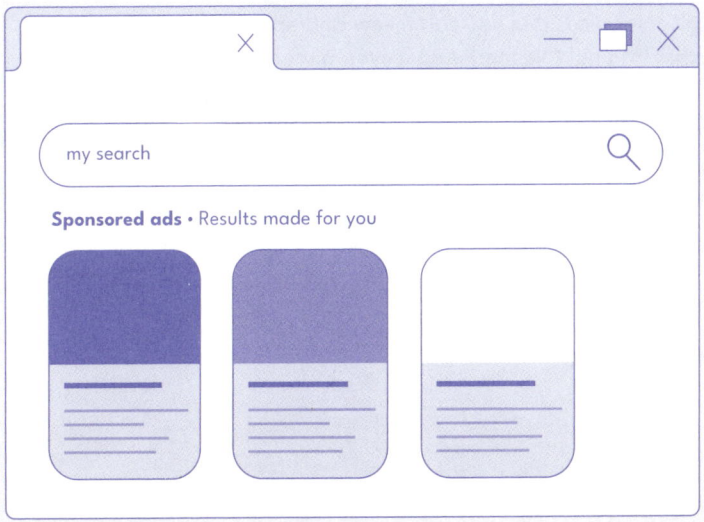

7. WHO IS TELLING THE STORY?

This is a question we encourage you to always consider when reading, watching, listening or consuming any type of news. It overlaps with our previous point about bias, but also goes to the idea of lived experience and the voices we choose to hear.

Let's use an example: when Kabul fell in 2021 (as you read about earlier in this book), if you turned on the TV, you would have likely seen foreign correspondents discussing the implications of the event.

On one channel, a panel of three male journalists talked through the developments over the course of a day as events unfolded. The reality of the situation, however, was (and remains) that those most impacted by the fall of Kabul were the women and girls of Afghanistan, who were looking at devastating restrictions on their lives, education and futures.

It's unlikely that most news outlets would have had any Afghan women, or anyone from Afghanistan, on their panels, and almost all of our media outlets need to do a better job of reflecting the people they seek to serve.

Of course, changing the face of the media is not something that is going to happen overnight. In the meantime, there are new, independent media publishers trying to empower fresh and diverse voices that you can follow and engage with. We suggest checking out Missing Perspectives, a media company for young women, which aims to spotlight diverse storytellers as well as to amplify female perspectives from around the world, which are often lost in traditional media.

A BIG QUESTION:
Do we need better representation on our screens?

Who gets to tell Australian stories? Does the diversity of our newsreaders, reporters and investigators matter? Absolutely. These people aren't just on our TVs, they're on the screens of our ever-present devices, in our social feeds and part of our dinner table conversations.

That's why it's so troubling that a 2022 Media Diversity Australia (MDA) report, 'Who Gets to Tell Australian Stories', found that First Nations Peoples and people from non-Anglo-Celtic cultural backgrounds remain significantly under-represented in news and current affairs coverage on Australia's free-to-air television networks.

MDA CEO Mariam Veiszadeh said the organisation works to 'hold up a mirror' to the industry's slow progress in 'creating a representative media landscape that looks and sounds more like Australia'.

The study measured the diversity of on-screen talent and executive leadership in the newsrooms of Australia's mainstream free-to-air television networks (i.e. the ABC, SBS, NITV and channels 7, 9 and 10). It also included a survey of staff and audience perceptions of diversity.

It considered four categories of cultural background, as set out by the 2016 and 2018 Leading for Change reports (commissioned by the Australian Human Rights Commission to analyse the cultural background of business leaders in Australia) – Anglo-Celtic, European, non-European and Indigenous.

In total, people from an Anglo-Celtic background made up:

- **78 per cent of on-air appearances on news and current affairs programs**
- **78 per cent of senior news leadership positions**
- **70 per cent of network board members**

Based on Census data, Anglo-Celtic people make up 54 per cent of the total population, meaning they are over-represented in every area of television media.

The representation of First Nations presenters had improved since the last time the study was conducted, in 2020. Two years later, First Nations journalists accounted for 5 per cent of total on-air appearances.

However, First Nations Peoples made up only 2.8 per cent of total presenters, which the report authors said showed representation was 'concentrated in a relatively small number of presenters and reporters'.

NITV, a part of SBS that specialises in First Nations reporting, had the highest representation. Channels 9 and 10 had improved since 2020. SBS had not improved, and the authors could not identify a single Indigenous presenter at Channel 7 in the period they were studying.

SBS was the only network with First Nations Peoples on its board, and NITV the only channel with them in senior news leadership positions.

European presenters made up 10 per cent of TV appearances, and people from non-European backgrounds made up 6 per cent. Both of these groups were, again, significantly under-represented: Europeans make up 18 per cent of the Australian population, and non-Europeans 25 per cent.

So, as the survey asked, does Australian news and current affairs represent the society they serve? The short answer is, not yet. But, as lead academic on the study Associate Professor Dimitria Groutsis observed, 'There has been some progress in parts of the media and an opportunity for Australian newsrooms to leverage best practice and become world leaders. This will not only attract more viewers, but will also yield economic dividends.'

A FINAL NOTE

If you've made it this far, you're now a bona fide Good News Consumer™ and are ready to take on the world.

The reality is, however, that in the years and decades to come, we are all going to have access to more information, not less. So our final piece of advice for you is that there are only so many news articles you can consume. It's impossible to stay across everything that happens in the world and, frankly, sometimes it's a mental-health burden to attempt to do so.

Instead, think about finding a way to consume the news that works for you. If you're a visual learner, perhaps watching a video explainer is the best way for you to understand a new topic. If you're more of a listener, find a podcast that you like (we've heard The Daily Aus podcast makes for great listening) and try to build that into your morning routine. It's all about leaning into your own consumption habits, figuring out what works for you and building your news diet around it.

One important thing to note is that there is a lot of bad news. And that's not exactly getting better. We often hear people saying things like 'I don't read the news because it's all too depressing' or 'I can't deal with all the bad news,' and believe us, we get it. It can be difficult.

Instead of using that as a reason to disengage completely, put in place measures to protect your mental health. These can look different for everyone. You could try adding sites that focus on 'good news' to your daily consumption habits. At TDA, we always publish a good news item in our daily wrap, and more and more other sites are also emphasising all the good being done in the world. Reading these stories and sharing them with friends can help mitigate how dark the news can be and can provide a gentler and more optimistic bright side.

It's now time for[...] forth on your ne[...] building on the [...] this book has pr[...] learning about [...] people in it and [...] As you undertak[...] we urge you to [...] questions, beca[...] there are **no silly**[...]

ou to go
s journey,
undations
vided and
r world, the
ow it works.
this journey,
ntinue to ask
se remember:
questions.

NOTES

To view the cited sources for each chapter, scan the QR code or go to thedailyaus.com.au/nsq-notes

IMAGE CREDITS

p. iv	Parliament House, Canberra	Andy Wang/Unsplash
p. v	Australian banknotes	RomanRa/Adobe Stock
	Solar panels and wind power generation equipment	hrui/Adobe Stock
p. vi	Invasion Day rally, Melbourne, 2021	Adam Calaitzis/Adobe Stock
	Tidbinbilla Deep Space Tracking Station	mastamak/Adobe Stock
p. vii	Planet Earth	FrameAngel/Adobe Stock

OUR POLITICAL SYSTEM

p. 26	Groups in different factions gathered around signs	galaira/Shutterstock
p. 32	Sir Edmund Barton	neftali/Shutterstock
	Ben Chifley	History and Art Collection/Alamy Stock Photo
	Sir Robert Gordon Menzies	Olga Popova/Shutterstock
p. 33	Harold Holt	GL Archive /Alamy Stock Photo
	Gough Whitlam	Keystone Press/Alamy Stock Photo
	Bob Hawke	Allstar Picture Library Ltd/Alamy Stock Photo
p. 34	Paul Keating	Vintage Image/Alamy Stock Photo
	John Howard	Allstar Picture Library Ltd/Alamy Stock Photo
	Julia Gillard	ausnewsde/Shutterstock

OUR CLIMATE

p. 79	Heads of state during arrival at COP21, Paris	Frederic Legrand – COMEO/Shutterstock
	Japanese prime minister Fumio Kishida delivers a speech at COP26 in Glasgow	Newscom/Alamy Stock Photo
p. 84	Sohal Tang (Acanthurus sohal) swimming	Zilvergolf/Adobe Stock
p. 93	Greta Thunberg	photocosmos1/Shutterstock
pp. 96–97	School Strike 4 Climate, 15 March 2019	Holli/Shutterstock

SOCIETY AND CULTURE

p. 125	Map of the United States	Vector FX/Adobe Stock
p. 137	'Queer and proud', Pride parade, July 2019	Delia Giandeini/Unsplash

SCIENCE AND TECHNOLOGY

p. 152	Evolution of the universe: cosmic timelines	Designua/Shutterstock
p. 154	James Webb Space Telescope infographic	© BBC
p. 156	LED panel	Adi Goldstein/Unsplash
p. 160	Jeff Bezos	lev radin/Shutterstock
	Bill Gates	Paolo Bona/Shutterstock
p. 161	Steve Jobs	Grey82/Shutterstock
	Elon Musk	Kathy Hutchins/Shutterstock
p. 162	Larry Page and Sergey Brin	dpa picture alliance/Alamy Stock Photo
	Mark Zuckerberg	Frederic Legrand – COMEO/Shutterstock

THE WORLD AROUND US

p. 187	World map	mas0380/Adobe Stock
p. 190	Wall Street sign	Lolo/Unsplash
p. 191	Arab Spring protest, Sana'a, Yemen, 11 October 2011	ymphotos/Shutterstock
p. 192	US president Donald Trump and vice-president Mike Pence, February 2019	History in HD/Unsplash
	Two million people protesting in Hong Kong, 16 June 2019	Manson Yim/Unsplash
p. 193	COVID-19	Martin Sanchez/Unsplash
	Standing with Ukraine, Manchester, UK, 5 March 2022	Ian Betley, Unsplash

ABOUT THE AUTHORS

Zara Seidler and Sam Koslowski are the co-founders of The Daily Aus. In only a few years, Sam and Zara have built a massive social media audience, two chart-topping podcasts, and successful newsletter and video channels in one of the hardest industries to crack – the news. After starting with a vision to bring their friends up to speed with the news, the pair became known for breaking down the complex ideas that sit behind current affairs with simplicity, respect and honesty. Now, they run the fastest-growing youth news company in Australia. They are business leaders, journalists, presenters and commentators, speaking to more than a million young Australians every month across social accounts, newsletters and podcasts. In 2022, Zara and Sam were listed in the *Forbes* 30 Under 30. It's a unique start-up story still unfolding.

thedailyaus.com.au
@thedailyaus

@zaraseidler
@samkoslowski

ACKNOWLEDGEMENTS

Writing a book was never part of the plan. The plan was to give this business-building thing a red-hot crack, and see if we could prove to ourselves – and Australia – that young people could be served with high-quality, trustworthy news content that didn't make the reader feel as if they were asking the wrong questions.

That plan is still in motion and far from finished. TDA started out as an experiment, and remains one. But now we have something else for our readers: a book. It has allowed us to create an archive and, hopefully, a helpful resource that brings together the day-to-day reporting we have so passionately brought our readers every day for the past six years.

The pace, franticness and fragility of the news cycle, let alone trying to build a sustainable business, doesn't make writing a book easy. That's why the biggest vote of thanks has to go to the wider TDA team, for their patience, optimism, enthusiasm, intelligence, innovation, energy, accuracy and trust.

To Tom, Lucy and Billi for their invaluable assistance in bringing this book together. We simply couldn't have got there without your help, and it exemplifies the spirit of teamwork we're trying to build at TDA.

To everyone else at TDA – Tara, Joe, James, Isaac, Nish, Sera, Daniel, Chloe, Sunny, Ninah and Emma – we love what we do because we get to do it with you. Seriously.

To Taylah Gray, whose work inspires us daily. Thank you for your generous time in advising and guiding us on the nuances of issues affecting First Nations Peoples.

To our partners, Olly and Montanna, the other founders. Thank you both for your unwavering support and love, and for being there to remind us that there's more to life than the news. Thank you for patiently enduring late nights and early mornings as news stories break, and for loving us despite the (sometimes dry) political chat. You are the two biggest champions of TDA and we treasure you for it.

To our families – thank you for instilling values of perseverance and curiosity into us. By providing us with a home base we know will always be there, you've allowed us to take risks and back ourselves. You encouraged us to take an odd obsession with news and the world around us, and make it our career.

To our investors, commercial partners, advisors and mentors – your support of a young business in a seriously challenging industry is brave, and we don't take it for granted. We feel so thankful that we have surrounded ourselves with people who support our vision and never make us compromise our core values of transparency and quality.

To Susan and Evi from Evi-O.Studio, thank you for bringing our words to life and making the sometimes mundane look exciting, fresh and new.

To Catherine, Kathryn, Izzy and Justin, and the entire team at Penguin Random House Australia, thank you for providing a steady hand through this daunting process. Sorry for not realising we can't stick to deadlines until we had already missed them. Thank you for indulging our curiosity and handling us with care!

And finally, to the TDA audience. Thank you for making this dream a reality. Keep asking questions, and we'll keep trying to answer them.

PENGUIN LIFE

UK | USA | Canada | Ireland | Australia
India | New Zealand | South Africa | China

Penguin Life is part of the Penguin Random House group
of companies whose addresses can be found
at global.penguinrandomhouse.com

First published by Penguin Life in 2023

Copyright © Zara Seidler and Sam Koslowski 2023

The moral right of the authors has been asserted.

All rights reserved. No part of this publication may be reproduced,
published, performed in public or communicated to the
public in any form or by any means without prior written
permission from Penguin Random House Australia Pty Ltd
or its authorised licensees.

Cover design, internal design, typesetting
and illustrations by Evi-O.Studio | Susan Le
© Penguin Random House Australia Pty Ltd
Author photograph by Martine Payne

Printed and bound in Australia by Griffin Press, an accredited
ISO AS/NZS 14001 Environmental Management Systems printer

 A catalogue record for this
book is available from the
National Library of Australia

ISBN 978 0 14377 728 1

penguin.com.au

We at Penguin Random House Australia acknowledge
that Aboriginal and Torres Strait Islander peoples are the
Traditional Custodians and the first storytellers of the lands
on which we live and work. We honour Aboriginal and Torres
Strait Islander peoples' continuous connection to Country,
waters, skies and communities. We celebrate Aboriginal and
Torres Strait Islander stories, traditions and living cultures;
and we pay our respects to Elders past and present.